Get the Life You Want!

101 Ways
to Use Your
Social IQ

Kristina Downing-Orr

Thorsons

Thorsons
An Imprint of HarperCollins*Publishers*
77-85 Fulham Palace Road,
Hammersmith, London W6 8JB

The Thorsons website address is: www.thorsons.com

First published by Thorsons 2000
1 3 5 7 9 10 8 6 4 2

© Kristina Downing-Orr 2000

Kristina Downing-Orr asserts the moral right to be
identified as the author of this work

A catalogue record of this book is
available from the British Library

ISBN 0 7225 3991 6

Printed and bound in Great Britain by
Omnia Books Limited, Glasgow

Contents

Part 2: Social Intelligence and the Art of Impressing Others

Acknowledgements

Many people have contributed to the completion of this book and I owe them my utmost thanks and gratitude. Wanda Whiteley, my editor at Thorsons, has been a true source of inspiration and creativity. Andrew Lownie, my literary agent, has been delightfully calm and serene, even in the most hectic of moments. Barbara Vesey, my copy editor, is sharp and thorough in her scrutiny of my manuscript. Most of all I'd like to thank all my corporate clients, who remind me every day of the countless reasons why human behaviour is so fascinating.

Part 1

From Drudgery to Dreams: Your Quest for Personal Success

Introduction: Success and Social Intelligence

What Does Success Mean to You?

Take a few moments now and think about your job and your life in general. Maybe you're trying to summon up the confidence to ask your boss for a pay rise or promotion. Perhaps you find yourself in a rut, stuck in a dead-end job without any real idea of how to go about exploring new and more rewarding opportunities. Or maybe you see other people in your company who are landing the types of positions that you want and know you would thrive at.

Now think about what it would mean to realize your ambitions. How about achieving everything you want from your life and shooting straight to the top of your chosen field? What do these words mean to you? Do they fill you with excitement at the prospect of dedicating your time and energy to achieving your goals? Or do you sit back, sigh and react in a 'if only' kind of way. Most of us have to work to survive. But we also have a choice. We can either spend our time stressed out and unhappy in a job situation which makes us feel unfulfilled, or we can look into ourselves, evaluate our talents and skills and go forward.

The choice is yours. It really is that simple. By stepping back, looking at your life and thinking about how you'd like to go forward, you are able to navigate. Once you take charge of that part of your life, you'll be in control of the rest.

As you proceed through this book, you will be equipped with the tools of success custom made to fit your life. This book is your recipe for fulfilment and success. I am going to help you reach your full personal and professional potential. Most of us are already equipped with the ability to achieve dreams or form new ones. We already have many of the skills needed for achievement and the capacity to seek new opportunities. What we tend to lack is guidance and help in defining and refining our goals. This book will show you how to foster and fine-tune your potential by instilling confidence in yourself and your ability to achieve your aims.

Maybe you've always known what you'd like to do and just need a push in the right direction, or perhaps you're someone who feels de-skilled and undervalued in your current job. In either case, frustration almost invariably sets in, making your situation more unsettling. This book will point you in the direction of success and fulfilment – however **you** define them. Throughout the book I've drawn on true-life 'case studies' of some of my clients, and events from my own life as well to illustrate the perils and ultimate satisfaction of striving for success. At the end of every chapter, there's a list of 'Top Tips' to help with everyday hurdles like how to create a winning CV, calling that person who can help you on your way, how to treat yourself well, and more.

Why Social Intelligence Can Help You Succeed

Climbing the ladder of success and achieving your goals require developing two main skills:

The **first** skill involves learning how to recognize, analyse and build on your own individual, unique talents, abilities and creativity to form goals you'd like to achieve.

The **second** is the ability to develop relationships with people who are influential in helping you to achieve these goals.

Developing your unique strengths and learning to attract the attention of influential people will be the tools of your success. No one becomes a star or leader in their field without the backing of agents, associates, publicists, producers, the media and more.

There is a widespread belief that intellectual and academic abilities automatically equal success. However, more recent findings are challenging this deeply entrenched view. In 1995 Daniel Goleman's bestselling book, *Emotional Intelligence*, introduced the concept that someone's ability to understand and interpret emotions is a far greater barometer of success than their native intelligence. He argued that emotions play a far greater role in thought, decision-making and personal achievement than previously thought. Based on breakthroughs in cognitive science, which highlighted recent discoveries of brain function, Goleman demonstrated how emotional intelligence can be nurtured and strengthened. While Goleman broadened our horizons by emphasizing the importance of other talents and skills besides intelligence, interpreting emotions is only part of the story. People also have to know how to act on them. Successful men and women also know the value of communicating with and winning the support of others in order to achieve their goals.

Let's take a look at your motivation and your commitment to making some important changes in your life. I can provide you with a step-by-step guide plus all the tricks of the trade, but not even the wisdom of Solomon will be any use unless you decide to do the work yourself. Making changes requires effort. A lot of effort. And time. So, before we go any further, answer the following questions:

- *Are you open to new approaches?*
- *Do you want a better quality of life?*
- *Do you want to spend your time working towards a goal that will challenge you and make the most of your skills?*
- *Do you have the resources and time to invest in yourself?*
- *Do you want to make more money?*
- *Is there a gap between what you're doing now and what you'd ideally like to do?*

If you've answered yes to these questions, then this book will work for you. If the negative replies have outstripped the positive ones, then here's more food for thought:

WHAT'S HOLDING YOU BACK?

Not enough time?
Too many commitments?
Fear of failure?
Worries that the process might be too difficult or demanding?
Low self-esteem?
All of the above?

That's OK. Don't worry. Most people can identify at least one or two barriers that prevent them from making changes. The important thing is to reflect upon and identify these obstacles so that you can act upon them. I encourage people to begin this process of reflection by completing the following exercise. It's called a **SWOT Analysis** because it asks you about your Strengths, Weaknesses, Opportunities and Threats that hold you back.

SWOT Analysis

MY STRENGTHS	MY WEAKNESSES
1.	1.
2.	2.
3.	3.
4.	4.
5.	5.

OPPORTUNITIES	THREATS
1.	1.
2.	2.
3.	3.
4.	4.
5.	5.

What were your positive and negative points? Did anything surprise you? Being honest with yourself, about your weaknesses as well as your strengths, is important. You'll need to know what assets you can build on and what limitations you will have to overcome in order to achieve your goals.

The SWOT Analysis is all about personal discovery, and I recommend you do the exercise every few months to monitor your goals and update your progress. But this is just the first step. Now it's time to think about taking stock of your life.

Top Tips for Success

Cocktail Party Confidence

1. Parties should be fun and entertaining, but mixing business with pleasure at a company do can be a nerve-wracking experience. And with good reason. Office etiquette still applies, so save kicking up your heels and tripping the light fantastic for another time.

2. Take your time getting ready for .
    bath, plan your wardrobe and think a**nce**
    the other guests.
3. Even if you're nervous, don't resort to liquid co m
    yourself one glass of wine. That's it. Otherwise you
    become a little *too* relaxed and find yourself telling the
    what you really think of her!
4. When you first enter the room, hesitate at the door for two
    or three seconds and compose yourself. Stand up straight
    and smile confidently. People will begin forming their
    impression of you at this point.
5. Black is the colour of sophistication and style, that's why so
    many people wear it. But you'll be noticed if you stand out.
    Wear a brightly coloured jacket or a patterned scarf –
    something that sets you apart.
6. Don't immediately rush over to someone you know. You'll
    look clingy and desperate. Instead, casually glance around
    the room and smile at the people you know. Then, slowly
    make your way towards them.

Just about everyone, at some time in life, thinks about making changes. Some people dream of drastic and extreme changes – like taking a job in a foreign country – while others are content with more modest pursuits – say, keeping fit. And although making changes, even ones for the better, may seem daunting, the process is also exciting, challenging and incredibly rewarding.

There is truly no greater sense of satisfaction than when you accomplish something you might not have otherwise dreamt possible. Sadly, many people remain hesitant about making changes, even though they would like to. What prevents them? What's stopping you?

Facing the Challenge of Change

You may not have realized it, but by taking the SWOT Analysis on page 15 you have now begun to take control over the course and direction of your life. It may seem obvious, but taking charge of the course and direction of your life is central to fulfilling your ambitions, to making your dreams come true. Often, though, when it comes to the day-to-day living of our lives, many people don't take any action over the course of their lives. They tend just to let it happen, to go with the flow, to see what comes up. In other words, they *wait* for opportunities to come to them. If a better job comes up, say, they take it. If a new relationship comes along, all the better, but if it doesn't, oh well. They stick with what they know.

As a psychologist, I find it inconceivable (in fact I'm shocked!) that people live their lives this way and expect to be fulfilled and happy. Sure, the opportunities may come along for some of us, but merely relying on the random whims of fate to bring us opportunity is only likely to bring disappointment in the long run. What's worse, by waiting for beneficial things to happen in your life, you have lost control. You are letting yourself become a passenger, passive, even at times a victim to the circumstances that surround you.

When you think about it, it does seem like an odd practice that we don't take more active involvement in planning the course of our lives. After all, in so many areas of our lives we do actually make quite a lot of effort. When we want a job, we tend to go out and apply for the one we want, plan out our CV or resume, make preparations for the interview. When we go on a trip, we first visit the travel agent, probably talk to friends and

family for destination recomme___ ___ions, pack and go to the
airport. We even make plan___ ___en we go grocery shopping.
Somehow, though, when ___ ___omes to *living our lives*, many just
somehow 'let it happe___ ___ithout much preparation or planning.
And this makes u___ ___nerable.

Life-line Exercise

Here's an exercise I want you to try. It will help you assess how
you feel about your life and the direction it's heading.

Imagine you have just been informed by your doctor that
you have only six months to live. How would you respond?
Obviously, not many people would be too happy at the prospect.
We start to grieve for what we'll miss in the lives of our family
and friends, and also we probably think about all the things we
have achieved or experienced in our lives, and, as well, all the
things we would have *liked* to have done, but somehow didn't.

The point of this exercise is to help you concentrate on your
accomplishments and achievements to date and to help you
determine how satisfied you are with the way things are pro-
gressing in your life.

Your Age___20___25___30___35___40___45___50___55___
60___65___70___75+

Look at the time line, above. I want you to think of this line
as representing your life in terms of years. Now, with a pen or
pencil I want you to draw a vertical line through your current
age. It doesn't have to be exact.

Next, I want you to begin to think about the general quality
of your life. Ask yourself the following questions:

1. *Are you generally pleased with the way your life has progressed?*
2. *Are there certain areas in your life that need changing?*
3. *What are your disappointments?*
4. *Are you looking forward to the future with enthusiasm?*
5. *Are there any goals that you would still like to achieve?*
6. *If you could do anything with your life what would it be?*
7. *What else do you want or need that will help make you feel complete?*
8. *Do you have any specific plans on how you would like to live your life?*

Assessing your life in this way provides a foundation from which we can formulate and then achieve our goals.

With these general thoughts in mind, I now want you to describe and appraise your **current view** of your life and **situation** – or **CVS,** as I call it. Just take a few moments to think about your current life and jot down any relevant descriptions about yourself and your life, such as hobbies, interests, relationships, your job. Remember there are no right or wrong answers.

MY CVS

1.
2.
3.
4.
5.
6.

7.

8.

9.

10.

Once you have completed this exercise you are now able to form better, more informed, more insightful evaluations about many different things in your life, which provide you both with a sense of satisfaction and with pointers to areas that need improvement. While we need to focus on the areas we would like to change and to improve, we can also draw an enormous amount of energy and strength from the things in our lives which we enjoy. Next, go back to the CVS and write down either 'satisfied' or 'unsatisfied' after each response.

Now, I want you to concentrate on those areas in your life you would like to improve, through a **better view of your situation,** or **BVS**. At this stage, don't worry about the practicalities of going about making these changes. For now I just want you to reflect on some changes in your life that would lead to improvement.

MY BVS

1.

2.

3.

4.

5.

6.

7.

8.

9.

10.

It doesn't really matter whether you came up with five answers for each column or ten. Some people can only come up with two or three at this stage. That's OK. I just want you to begin assessing your current life and thinking about possible directions for change and improvement. That is the point of the CVS and the BVS. And, as with the SWOT, the CVS and the BVS, when regularly updated, help us define our goals and give our lives direction and purpose.

Top Tips for Success

Keeping the Boss Smiling

Impressing the boss will be a whole lot easier, if you watch out for bad habits.

1.   Don't be late. It doesn't matter if the train's been delayed or your dog keeps getting loose. If you're always the last one to arrive in the morning and chronically keeping your colleagues waiting, you'll come across as inconsiderate and unreliable. Your co-workers will start to resent you and your boss won't even consider you for promotion. Figure in some extra time in your daily schedule and you'll be on time.

2. Put off putting it off. No more procrastination. If you're someone who tends to do everything at the last minute, you're running the risk that the job might not get done. Even if you manage to beat the deadline, is it worth the stress? Have a look at your workload. Are you taking on too much work? Do you feel overwhelmed by responsibility? Are you just plain bored? In any event, the job will need to get done. Break the tasks into small, manageable chunks and complete one of those a day. Writing a list of things you need to accomplish will also help with your organization.

3. Maintain focus. Do you become easily distracted? Do you daydream frequently? Do you need to be reminded of important dates, names and other relevant details? If so, you run the risk of appearing disorganized and undisciplined. Prepare for meetings, keep track of appointments and stay on the ball.

4. Don't eat food at your desk. Not only could you spill the guacamole all over important documents, but your food could stink out the office all day.

5. Never swear or behave crudely. You might have had the best sex of the decade. Your PMT might be driving you crazy. You could have just finished reading the latest article on female orgasms. Are these appropriate conversations for the workplace? No. Save them for the pub.

6. Don't lose sight of your priorities. If you're someone who takes on too much work but never gets anything done, you might develop a reputation as someone who can't prioritize. Allocate an hour every morning to identify the most urgent tasks and limit yourself to accomplishing them.

7. Don't even think about spreading office gossip – no matter how juicy!
8. Don't put yourself down, even if it's false modesty. If you undervalue your work, others will too.

Looking at the Present
with a Focus on the Future

Thinking about your goals is only one part of the plan. You now have to plan to *act*. A lot of people lose confidence at this stage, however. That's because making changes, even for the better, is a daunting experience. Unfortunately, though, people often lose confidence and motivation when faced with the challenge of putting their plans into action. They lose their bottle and delay achieving their goals. They tell themselves the time isn't right or that they haven't enough skill, or come up with a thousand other excuses.

When faced with the insecurities of change and the unknown, the comfort zone is usually the most attractive option. But it doesn't have to be. You can overcome these anxieties. In fact, these are usually the worst obstacles to overcome, so once you face up to these worries or doubts, you'll be well on your way to achieving your goals.

What's Holding You Back?

Is It Fear?

Fear is the great disabler. Fear of the unknown, fear of change, fear of making ourselves look stupid or foolish, fear of being afraid and unsettled – for all kinds of reasons, fear holds us back.

When it comes to feeling fear, you have two choices. You can either avoid confronting your anxieties or you can face them head on. I know the temptation is often to run away, but facing up to your fears is not so daunting. Really.

Every new experience and challenge will produce anxiety and fear. That's because we, as humans, are biologically predisposed to developing symptoms of anxiety in new and potentially threatening situations. It's in our genes, and these feelings of distress are normal. But they don't have to disable you. In fact, I would wager a bet that you've felt fear and anxiety when encountering new and unfamiliar situations lots of times. I would also wager that these distressing feelings disappeared and you regained confidence once you'd become familiar with that situation.

Think about such a situation in your own life. Perhaps it was the first day of a new job, a blind date, approaching the gates of a new school, visiting a foreign country, meeting potential in-laws or buying a new house. The list is endless, and they're all stressful situations. However, after a month at the new job,when the blind date turns into a relationship or once you've made some friends at the new school, etc., the feelings of distress fade away. The funny thing is, though, once a situation becomes familiar to us we tend to forget that we were ever anxious in the first place.

Do You Feel Incapable of Success?

Some people tell me that they are just incapable of succeeding or achieving anything. These people tell me 'I never succeed at anything I do,' 'I've always been a failure, so I'll always be a failure.' Unfortunately, because they always accentuate their failures in life, these people selectively forget their accomplishments.

Sound familiar?

Now, with these thoughts in mind I want you to reflect for a moment on your life. Jot down, on the list below, as many of your accomplishments and achievements that you can think of. Take about three or four minutes for this exercise.

My Accomplishments

1.
2.
3.
4.
5.
6.
7.
8.
9.
10.

Don't worry if you didn't list 10 achievements and accomplishments. A shorter list will do. Likewise, if you have a whole series of successes to jot down, please feel free to extend the list and write them all down on a separate piece of paper. Most of us are not rocket scientists or Nobel prize winners, so don't be too harsh on yourself. If you are like most people you will be able to list some accomplishments, I'm sure. Finishing school or university, getting married, being promoted at work, cultivating a beautiful garden – all of these are accomplishments to be proud of. And I am sure there will also be certain things that you haven't done, but would still like to – have children, travel around the world, join the Peace Corps or VSO, learn to juggle, whatever. In the following spaces below, write down some of the achievements you would still like to accomplish. And please don't worry at this stage about the practicalities of how actually to achieve them.

What I Hope to Achieve

1.
2.
3.
4.
5.
6.
7.
8.
9.
10.

For you to feel successful, for you to excel at some goal or achievement, for you to feel personally fulfilled and experience the joys and benefits of personal growth, you alone must decide what you want out of life.

The second point of this exercise is to offer you proof, demonstrable evidence, that you also have some past history of success and achievement. Many people, particularly those who are feeling insecure or depressed or have low self-esteem, believe that they are unable to accomplish or achieve anything, that they are incapable of success. The above list will serve as a reminder to you that you have the capability to achieve those goals in your life that are important to you, because you have already demonstrated resourcefulness, efficiency, discipline, planning, initiative, creativity, time-management and all the other countless requirements that go along with achieving goals.

When many of my clients begin reflecting on their accomplishments and achievements, some still voice reservations at this point. This isn't because they have never accomplished or achieved anything. Far from it. Many are high achievers. The first problem is that many don't appreciate the value of their achievements. It is a perverse logic that to some people if they have succeeded or have something, then that success or achievement loses its value. Any time you feel that you are incapable of achieving, I want you immediately to go back to the list on page 28 and read again about all your achievements. If after reading this list you still don't feel convinced, I want you to look at the list *again*. If you are like most people, you may not feel that your accomplishments have really been that significant. You went to secondary school/passed your driving test/became a solicitor or gourmet chef, so what? If you are still not convinced of the worthiness of these achievements, set your thoughts on two things:

First, think of someone you know or have heard of who hasn't managed to achieve the same goals. This will be relatively easy to do, I assure you. I am sure there are many close friends and relatives who marvel at some of your talents. I, for one, because I have no innate ability to cook, am always amazed when friends manage to throw together a gourmet meal without much effort. The most I can make is a booking at a restaurant! So, while cooking or baking may seem trivial and routine to some, others will consider it a great talent – as Laura, one of my clients, found out. After a divorce that left her self-esteem in ruins, Laura used to come to sessions with me and would occasionally bring along some delicious home-made chocolate cake. The cake was so good that I suggested she think about making it professionally. Why not try, I asked her. After a little prompting Laura contacted a few bakeries and gourmet coffee shops. Within a few months Laura had so many regular orders she was able to quit her job – a job she'd hated. Now, Laura had had no idea that this cake, something she made as a hobby just to please herself, would generate so much interest and eventual income – until, that is, she was able to see the value in something she could achieve. So, others' appreciation for what you've managed to do will certainly demonstrate the value of your success.

Another thing you can do if you feel that your list of accomplishments is unimpressive is to say to yourself, 'I accomplished all these goals without consciously being aware of what I was doing, that I was actually accomplishing something. Imagine what I can do when I *consciously decide* to achieve a specific goal?' In many of the goals we have achieved – school, college, getting a job – because other people are doing them and they are expected of us, we don't tend to appreciate that they require discipline, strategy, creativity, energy, commitment, drive, resourcefulness and countless other qualities necessary for success. If you accomplished these goals without being consciously aware of the steps involved, you can set your mind and energy to just about anything.

Do You Feel You Don't Deserve a Better Life?

Some people feel that they don't deserve success or happiness. Sometimes they believe that they are unworthy of the rewards that success brings. In many instances, because they belittle their talents and abilities, they feel that true achievement is the preserve of the lucky few. In either case, this low self-esteem is usually the result of negative views that they have picked up from others.

We live in a world with a lot of negative thinking. I call this the **big can't do**. I, like most people, experience this almost daily. When we want to try out new ideas or discuss tentative plans, people confront us with all kinds of reasons why we can't. Once you're more experienced in breaking out and trying new things, however, you'll be more resilient to the 'big can't do'. And once you've developed this confidence, you'll be open to the rewards of success. Read on.

Top Tips for Success

Phone Call Finesse

1. Always return calls by the next working day.

2. Even if you're returning a call, always introduce yourself and remind the other person why you're contacting them. This will help spare their embarrassment and yours!

3. Make sure you have a pen and some paper handy, in case you need to write down information. The other person may become annoyed if left hanging while you go in search of a message pad.

4. Refrain from taking phone calls when you're in a meeting. You'll appear rude and the interruption will be distracting. If you absolutely, positively have to take an important call, then keep it brief. You can call the person back once the meeting's over.

5. Have an outline handy of all the essential points you need to cover. That way you won't forget anything important and won't need to chase the other person up.

6. When you're ready to make the call, go and find a quiet room where you're less likely to be disturbed. Make sure the television and the radio are turned off.

7. Smile when you dial and continue smiling the whole time you're speaking. Your voice will sound much more relaxed.

8. If you get an answerphone, don't be thrown off. Leave a message and speak slowly. Always, always say you'll ring them back. This will keep you in control. Write down ahead

of time what you're going to say, including a list of
questions if you're trying to find out about, for example, a
job. Practise reading what you've written so it sounds
natural.

Working to Live or Living to Work? It's Your Call

Formulating goals and making decisions about your career isn't an easy process, because there is no one recipe for success. Making decisions is made more difficult because, by choosing one particular pathway to follow, we are automatically rejecting others. What if we make the wrong decision? How can we ensure we're making the right choice?

Finding Meaning

One way to ensure you are making the right decisions for you is to develop a sense of purpose and find meaning to your life. For thousands of years, people have been questioning the meaning of life because it is human nature to want to find out if our lives have some kind of meaning. Who are we? Why are we here? Are we just an accident of evolution? Questions such as these are central to this process. Meaning can help to supply us with a sense of involvement in our lives, and reassures us that we are in some way significant. That we are important. That we matter. That our position on earth has some sort of relevance.

Think about the importance of purpose and meaning in life for a moment. What, for you, gives your life purpose and meaning?

This is a question which only you can answer. But the answers are within you, even if they may not seem immediately obvious.

Think about this story for a moment. It comes from a man named Yalom.

Imagine there is a happy group of fools working together in a field. Throughout the entire day, their task is to carry some heavy bricks in an open field. They transport the bricks down one end of the field and stack them up to form a wall. As soon as they are finished constructing the wall, they then proceed to dismantle it. They then carry all the bricks down to the other end of the field and reconstruct the wall.

The happy group of fools continue building and dismantling this wall, without stopping, every day of every year.

One day, however, one of the fools stops long enough to think about what he is doing. He begins to wonder what purpose there is in carrying the bricks, building the wall, only to dismantle it again.

And from that instant on he is not quite as happy any more.

I am the moron who wonders why he is carrying bricks.

Do you ever wonder why you go through all the trouble and

effort involved in your life? The importance of finding meaning in our lives is that it gives us a spirit of vitality instead of apathy, passivity and alienation. It gives us – and this is crucial to finding happiness – a sense of fulfilment and success.

Finding Your Purpose

- *Are you actively involved in all aspects of your life – your emotions, thoughts, actions and behaviours?*
- *Do you want to live life to the full?*
- *Do you find enjoyment in life?*
- *Do you accept that your values and goals are likely to change as you grow older?*
- *Do you lead an active life?*
- *Do you enjoy creative ventures and new experiences?*

Perhaps you were never meant to be a rocket scientist, world leader or famous performer. Maybe your purpose in life stems from spending time with your family and friends, or being a great teacher, or developing a talent for watercolours. The choice is up to you. You, and only you, can decide what gives your life meaning.

Top Tips for Success

Voice Mail Confidence

Most of us rely on voice mail to contact and communicate with clients and colleagues. Speak with confidence and you'll convey a favourable impression. Hesitate and stumble over your words and you'll look incompetent. Remember, your voice mail is quite literally your calling card!

1. Change and update your voice-mail message on a regular basis. It will demonstrate to your callers that you actually do pick up your messages and are on top of things.
2. Make sure your messages are brief and to the point.
3. Make sure you speak slowly and clearly, repeating any important contacts or telephone numbers.
4. If you will be away for an extended period of time, be sure to record a return date and the name of the person who will be covering your calls while you are away.

That Dream Job Is
Yours for the Taking

I am now going to ask you to dream for a moment. Dreams are important because they inspire our goals and give us encouragement and the strength to persevere.

I would like you to take a few moments to do another exercise. This is a visualization exercise so it is best done in a quiet, comfortable relaxing room where you won't be disturbed. It won't take too long, probably about 10 minutes at the most.

Read through the exercise first.

When you are seated comfortably in a chair, I want you to close your eyes and think about how you would like to live your life. In this visualization, I would like you to start off by completing the phrase '*I want* . . . . . .' Remember, it's not what you feel you *should* want, but what you *actually* want that's important here. Just let your mind and imagination flow freely, so that you can come up with a picture of your preferred lifestyle. Imagine, really visualize, that you are doing precisely whatever it is you've always dreamed of doing, that you are the person that you have always dreamed of being. In this visualization, focus only on the positive aspects, the successes. Sweep from your mind any hint of negativity or failure.

Now, still using your imagination I want you actually to place yourself in your dream and observe yourself living out your goal. Experience what it feels like to achieve that goal and all the sensations that go along with it: confidence, success, energy, dynamism, self-respect, courage.

If you are having some trouble imagining your perfect life and lifestyle, here are two helpful suggestions to think about. The first thing is to accept that our dreams and goals have to be realistic. This, of course, is not to say that you shouldn't aim for the highest possible achievements, but if you are 45 years old and you dream of winning at the Wimbledon finals without so much as having picked up a racket in 10 years, your dream is unlikely to come true. And you will be disappointed. Stick to aims and ambitions that are within your grasp.

Identifying Your Dream Job

What Did You Want to Be When You Grew Up?

What careers captured your attention when you were 5, 10, 15? Were there any particular games or hobbies that so engrossed you that the time just sped by? What were the qualities of these games or hobbies that so appealed to you? Think about the activities that made you feel happy and inspired; these will point you in the direction of the right career choice for you.

Jessica was a client of mine who was a successful journalist, but she felt unfulfilled and found the pressures of writing daily news stories becoming a grind. We explored potential career choices and I asked her what her first career ambition had been. She said she had always been interested in anthropology and had initially become a journalist so she could travel and write about global cultures. Her job had become mundane because she wasn't really interested in reporting news and politics. Jessica decided to pursue a degree in anthropology and combine her journalistic and academic interests.

If You Could Wave a Magic Wand and Have All the Money in the World, How Would You Spend Your Day?

Monica was training to be a doctor. From a very early age she decided that she wanted a career in medicine, because she wanted to help people. Monica went to all the right schools, worked hard and passed all the right exams, dedicated years of her life to her training and realized she hated every minute of it. Monica found the profession conservative and chauvinistic. She found her patients unwilling to comply with her advice and ungrateful for her efforts. More importantly, Monica felt stifled in terms of her creativity. A talented artist, Monica no longer had time to draw and paint due to the long hours on the wards.

Burnt out and fed up, Monica decided that a career change was necessary for her sanity, but felt guilty about abandoning her medical career. I asked Monica what she would do with her life if she could do absolutely, positively anything. Money, guilt, training and parental pressures aside, Monica told me she'd like to be an artist. We talked through the practicalities and Monica began applying for different jobs. She began accepting commissions to illustrate medical textbooks, and then she landed her dream job – designing programmes for video games. Three years on, Monica has never been happier and has no regrets about giving up her medical career.

Ask Yourself What's Really Important to You

Money? Free time? Pursuing something creative? Helping others? Living abroad? Re-acquainting yourself with your passions will motivate you to make the right choices for you.

I have a friend, Mike, whose just mad about films and knew very early on that he wanted to be a producer. He works 18-hour days, seven days a week and his travelling commitments are nothing short of gruelling, but he loves what he does. He's now in his mid-thirties and has just landed a big television deal with one of the major networks. But, for Mike, the money's not important. He just wants to make films.

Think About What Your Natural Role Is with Other People

What are your roles in life? Are you the carer? The motivator? The leader? The teacher? Adventurer? Which of these roles do you find most fulfilling? Least fulfilling?

What About Your Achievements and Goals So Far?

Take a minute to identify which of your achievements and goals in life you have found most personally and professionally rewarding.

Top Tips for Success

Making Contacts Can Make All the Difference

1. In order to impress influential people, you need to appear self-confident. Pay attention to grooming, clothes, eye contact and your posture – all will give the impression you're worth their time.

2. Learn to feel comfortable in the company of power. If you're intimidated by expensive restaurants, exclusive clubs or powerful people, then change. If you want to be successful, get used to the accoutrements of wealth and influence.

3. Hang out in places where you're likely to meet powerful people. Many wannabe actors, for example, work as waiters in restaurants where producers and directors frequently dine. Think about joining a gym, club, political party or professional association; you'll increase your contact with the power merchants.

4. You're at the right place, mingling with the right people, so be brave and make your move. Don't waffle. Get straight to the point. And, make that contact.

5. Always have a supply of business cards handy. And don't be shy about asking someone else for theirs. Then, call them straightaway.

The Value of Work Ethics

Identifying your values and developing your own personal integrity will help you define your goals. Maybe you're the type of person with a strong sense of moral outrage when it comes to social injustice, the environment and the welfare of others. Perhaps your concerns are more focused on your own personal actions and behaviours. Whatever your personal ethics, you can rest assured that they will have an impact on the work you do and the career decisions you make.

I have a friend, Lisa. On paper, her life looked impressive and gratifying. She was vice-president at her company, her salary was in six figures and she made a regular habit of month-long holidays in the Caribbean. Nevertheless, she was absolutely miserable.

Lisa began to realize that she was unfulfilled in her career. Before Lisa entered corporate life she'd been working towards a

*teaching qualification, but let herself be convinced by her
father that she could earn more money working in a big
company. At first she liked the challenge, and her hard work
and enthusiasm quickly paid off. But over the years Lisa
realized something else. She was tired of getting up at five
every morning and coming home at nine. She was fed up with
being bad-tempered and stressed, of having employees call her
at home. She began to think about her original ambitions of
entering the teaching profession and concluded that she
wanted to dedicate her life to helping others.*

*Making the decision to leave her high-salaried, prestige job
was not easy. Lisa was the principal breadwinner in her family,
and returning to teaching meant drastic changes to her
lifestyle. She also experienced the disapproval of her father,
who was convinced Lisa had rocks in her head for wanting to
give up her position. However, returning to teaching was the
best decision Lisa ever made. She feels her skills and talents
make a difference to the community and are appreciated.*

In all aspects of our lives it is important to live by our *own* code
of ethics. In theory this sounds easy, but it's not. We can risk
isolation from our peers and disapproval from those we love.
However, if we live by someone else's values, we end up living
a lie.

Other people will also judge you by your personal ethics,
and this can also affect your career. Take the following example.

*A client of mine called Amelia had been working for an
advertising agency for several years, but felt she had difficulties
getting along with her colleagues both socially and professionally.*

Although she described the office as friendly, Amelia always felt left out. People were cordial to her, but cold, and she had no idea why. Amelia did everything possible to try to make friends and develop good relationships with her colleagues, but the more she tried, the more distant people would appear. Since she didn't have a clue as to why she was being frozen out, we decided to try to find out together.

Amelia gave the following example of a typical work scenario. She told me that she would often try to be helpful if someone was having problems at work. One day, she came across two fellow employees who were arguing about the details of an advertising campaign they were working on. Amelia thought she might be able to help out and approached each woman separately to offer her support. However, while listening sympathetically to one colleague complain about the other, Amelia was still eager to maintain good relations with both women.

Suddenly, I could see the problem. I asked Amelia if she found herself agreeing with the negative comments each of the women were making. She confirmed that she was. Amelia didn't realize it, but by offering support and sharing negative information about both women, she left herself open to being seen as two-faced and insincere. Her colleagues were thus suspicious of her motives and her friendly overtures. And they'd obviously decided not to have anything to do with her.

It took Amelia a little time to grasp this concept. While she thought she was showing support, others viewed her actions as disingenuous. Once she realized how others perceived her actions, Amelia modified her behaviour and her colleagues began to respond to her more positively.

Developing Your Own Personal Code

As we have seen from the examples outlined above, developing a personal integrity code is very important. Matching your career choice to your values and ethics will ensure that you feel fulfilled and satisfied. You will also gain the respect of those with whom you work.

Step One: *Write down 10 ways in which you think you demonstrate integrity both towards yourself and others.*

Step Two: *Now write down 10 ways in which you feel your integrity needs improvement.*

Step Three: *Next, write down all the things you need in your life to make you happy and fulfilled.*

Step Four: *Finally, piece all these different elements together and, in a few sentences, write down your own personal and professional goals. This is your own **personal mission statement**, which you can refer back to for motivation.*

@@@@@@@@@@@@@@@@@@@@@@@@@@@@

Top Tips for Success

Conversations with Confidence

1. Speak up, don't be shy. Never ever say, 'I know this may sound stupid, but ...' Even if your opinion is well-informed and intelligent, opening gambits like this will only give the impression that you lack confidence.

2. If you're interested in joining in on a conversation but haven't been able to get a word in edgeways, here's how to interrupt with aplomb. First, acknowledge the previous speaker and then launch right in. 'John, that is a fascinating point and I'd just like to say . . .'

3. Asking someone about a topical news item, the latest film or novel, or even their recent holidays is a good way of getting a conversation off the ground.

4. Focus all your attention on the person you're speaking with. Never look over their shoulder or appear distracted, you'll come across as rude and bored.

5. Be discreet and diplomatic. When speaking to someone you've never met before, stick to light-hearted conversation. Otherwise you might later find out you've been slagging off the boss to his wife all evening. Not good.

6. Try to limit the discussion to positive or neutral topics of conversation. Save your negative thoughts for your friends.

7. You've been delayed. Your secretary called in sick and you've had to work late. Then you had to wait 45 minutes for a bus and got caught in a downpour. And, wouldn't you know it? You lost your wallet somewhere along the way. I don't care what kind of hellish day you've had. You'll come across as a complainer if you whine about your experiences. Save your rantings until you get home.

8. To encourage conversation, don't give out too much information about yourself. Be deliberately vague and other people will ask you questions. 'Where are you from?' 'Scotland.' 'Where? Glasgow? Edinburgh?' 'No, the Highlands.' 'I've been to Inverness. Is that near your home?' Etc.

9. It used to be considered 'bad form' to ask people what they did for a living, but now it's an acceptable icebreaker.

Making Decisions with Confidence

The most successful and fulfilled people are those who believe wholeheartedly that they are masters of their own destiny. Of course, all of us live in a world in which certain restrictions and limitations are imposed on us, by our family, the government, the community in which we live. We have to wear certain types of clothes to work. Most of us resist the urge to burst into song on a crowded train. And most of us understand that it isn't even always acceptable to tell the truth, because we might hurt someone's feelings if we do.

We can exert quite a lot of autonomy over our thoughts, emotions, behaviours, actions and attitudes. Having the power to initiate thoughts and opinions demonstrates that we are autonomous. In fact, just believing that you are autonomous and that you actually have the ability to develop autonomy is the most important step in taking charge of your life and making your dreams come true.

It can be a bit scary and intimidating to think about taking the first stab at independence, but with practice you will find that the process becomes a lot easier. You can begin by reflecting on your own life. Think about all those areas in which you feel you have some sense of control and autonomy. Also, think about those areas in your life in which you would like to exert more autonomy.

Once you have thought about your life in this way for a while, here is a very simple exercise that will help show you that you can very easily create new actions, and will demonstrate to you that not only are new actions possible, but you have actively taken a role in creating them for yourself.

Step One

Think about an activity that you rarely or never do. It doesn't have to be a daunting or elaborate one. In fact, make it as simple as possible. Travelling by public transport, giving a talk on a hobby or a matter of local interest, visiting a retirement community, investigating courses at a local community college, going to the theatre, visiting Paris, making initial inquiries about a job – the list is endless. The point here is just to THINK of something new that you have never done before.

Next, I want you to then think about all the steps involved in preparing for this activity. What plans would you have to make ahead of time?

Step Two

Now that you have come up with an idea, I want you to imagine in your mind's eye actually going out and doing or taking part in this activity. For example, envision yourself sitting on a commuter train, making a speech in front of an audience, sitting in a French Literature class, watching a play, taking the lift to the top of the Eiffel Tower, calling a human resources manager, etc. Really focus on all the things involved, the other people who are present, what you are wearing, what they are wearing, what you are saying and doing and how the other people are responding to you.

Also, concentrate on all the emotions being generated within you when you are imagining yourself participating in this activity.

Step Three

Now that you have concentrated on this new activity I would like you to go out and do it. And as you are actually physically participating in this activity, I want you to become consciously aware that you alone are responsible for initiating, planning, preparing and doing this activity. More importantly, as you participate in this activity I want you to stress to yourself over and over again that *you alone* have chosen to do this, and that you, yourself, have created something, some new action or behaviour which you had not experienced before.

Really concentrate, too, on all the emotions that you feel at this moment. Confidence? Excitement? Achievement?

Step Four

You can do this exercise over and over again with things you would like to do, and in doing them also attempt to develop a more conscious sense of creative autonomy in your own life.

I am sure you will be able to appreciate the benefits of this exercise. Most people don't realize that they can develop a strong sense of autonomy of thought and action. Once you become more comfortable with the idea of generating new thoughts and actions, the more confident you will be in making choices and creating new opportunities that will allow you to reach your goals.

Top Tips for Success

Essentially, Organized

1. Make a list of everything you need to accomplish for the day. It's a real sense of achievement when you draw a line through a task you've completed.
2. Think up ways of saving time. Bulk buy. Shop on the internet. Use your lunch hour to catch up on work or return calls.
3. Unless there's something that absolutely, positively has to be done, don't commit yourself. You'll only feel stressed and resentful.
4. Organize your files and records so you can locate the information when you need it. I recommend those file holders with lots of pockets. They don't take up much space and you can keep all your paperwork in one place.

5.   Know your limits and make sure you understand your cut-off points. With endless responsibilities, family commitments, friends, socializing, keeping fit, etc., etc., we need more than 24 hours in a day. You'll only wear yourself out if you're not careful. When you've had enough, don't push yourself any further.

6.   At the start of every week, prioritize what you need to do. I make a list of the top 10 things that need to get done and organize them in order of importance. If I complete the top five, then I'm happy. If anything important is still outstanding, I transfer it to the following week.

7.   Sometimes we can't predict what we need to prioritize. Emergencies crop up. Your boss unexpectedly 'reminds' you of some project that's due, even if this is the first time you've heard of it. Plan for the unexpected and be prepared to juggle your demands.

8.   Accept that your desk isn't ever going to be completely clear at the end of the day. Worrying about what you've still got to do is counter-productive and will only place undue pressure on your shoulders. Focus on what you've achieved.

9.   Ask people to prioritize their communications to you. I have a system of Urgent, Important, or Routine. However, most people I work with will insist that their request *is* urgent or important – even when it's not. Once you find out the specifics of what's required, you'll probably have to negotiate.

10.   Don't let things pile up. Do a little bit of something every day. Housework and other chores can accumulate really quickly. However, spending 15 minutes a day tidying up or doing the laundry will keep things manageable.

Are You Compatible with Your Career? Your Personality Profile

There is a saying I always share with my clients when they come to me eager to discuss their dream job. 'Be careful what you want out of life; you might just get it.'

A dream job can turn into a nightmare scenario, and many disappointed people have said they didn't realize what they were getting themselves into when making career changes. So it's important you not only investigate the necessary qualifications, time commitments and weigh up the pros and cons of your new career choice, you also need to find out if your personality suits the job.

The match between personality and career choice is frequently ignored, but think about the consequences of an extrovert who thrives on the company of others stuck in an office on her own all day. Or how about the introvert who prefers to work in the background being forced to stand up and give presentations to prospective clients? Professional satisfaction, I think not.

Remember, there is no **one** personality type that guarantees success. The key, however, is to match your personality to the requirements of your career choice. To find out a little bit about how your personality can help determine a good fit with your career choice, ask yourself the following questions:

Organized vs Spontaneous Personalities

1. *Do you like it when things are well-organized and structured so that you know what is expected of you most of the time?*
   YES/NO
2. *Do you prefer to do things spontaneously and believe that too much organization is unnecessary, even stifling?*
   YES/NO

If you described yourself as someone who likes to be **organized**, then you can use this knowledge in your choice of career. If you answered yes to the first question, then you are more likely to favour jobs and other situations in which planning and schedules are well-maintained. In fact, you might become stressed or anxious when something unpredictable happens.

In contrast, if you described yourself as more **spontaneous**, you would probably prefer to be more flexible and less rigid in your work situations. A structured, well-organized environment will probably become a dull routine and you would most likely need to find variety throughout your work day.

Next, we can also find out about the ways in which you gather in and absorb information. People tend to be either **factual** or **intuitive**.

Factual vs Intuitive Personalities

1. *Before making a decision, would you prefer to have all the details?*
   YES/NO
2. *Before making a decision, do you tend to look at the wider picture?*
   YES/NO

Detail-oriented or **factual** people are unlikely to let anything slip their eye, but they also have to take care that they are not sacrificing details for other things. In work situations, if your job requires that you work on projects that seem vague and unstructured and focus on general aims and conclusions, you might feel lost.

If you are the type of person where the broader picture is of more interest, then you are an **intuitive** person, because you will most likely want to investigate different possibilities and look at things from many different angles. While this is important for generating ideas, you might miss an important detail. In the work situation, with this kind of person, you may find that having to work out the minute details stifles your imagination and is boring.

We then could find out more about the ways you make decisions once all the information has been gathered. When it comes to making decisions, people tend to be either **analytical** or **sympathetic** in their approach.

Analytical vs Sympathetic Personalities

1. *When it's time to make a decision, would you describe yourself as logical?*
    YES/NO
2. *Or do you tend to be sympathetic, by which we mean rely on your emotions?*
    YES/NO

If you are **logical**, you will probably prefer to be in situations which require objectivity or working with numbers. Conversely, if you are **sympathetic** and are compassionate to other people's views on life, then you should investigate careers where you would be working with and assisting people.

Next, we can also find out your preferred strategies for working with people. Some people have to work uninterrupted, almost in isolation, while others would go mad if they were spared the company of others throughout the day.

Extrovert vs Introvert Personalities

1. *Do you prefer to work independently and on your own?*
    YES/NO
2. *Do you prefer to work as part of a team?*
    YES/NO

Some people need to be surrounded by activity and thrive on interaction with their colleagues. Others prefer to be left to their own devices and to get on with the task at hand without interruptions.

Take a moment to jot down which of these general categories you identify most with. This will help when we come to the next step, combining personality traits.

Combining Personality Traits

The categories described above represent extremes in personality; you will probably find you have elements of many different traits. Identifying these different combinations will also be useful in your career choice. Here's how.

When people are both **factual** and **organized**, they are likely to feel most comfortable in situations where accuracy and care are necessary.

Factual and **spontaneous** people tend to be energetic and like activity. They will be happy in those jobs which require instant action and the generation of immediate solutions.

Intuitive and **analytical** people are creative and very good at generating ideas. They prefer to work in situations where a goal has been identified, and like to come up with their own creative solutions.

Intuitive and **sympathetic** people make good teachers or advisers, because they want to help other people achieve.

Are You Compatible with Your Career?

Finding Your Match

Questions like these can help you seek the kind of job you like, and avoid those work situations which are unsuitable and are at odds with your personality. Try the following exercise. Think about your current job situation, or maybe even your entire career history, in terms of your personality characteristics. In what ways does your job match your personality? In what ways is there a mismatch?

Top Tips for Success

Treat Yourself Well

1. Don't neglect your appearance. Personal style and grooming are as essential to the boardroom as flip charts and Mont Blanc pens. Keep a make-up bag in your desk, have your shoes shined regularly and pay frequent visits to the manicurist.

2. Recharge your batteries. Whether you book yourself a weekly massage, take walks through the park or meet up with an old friend to catch up on the gossip, it's important that you distract your mind from all your demands. You'll feel energized and better equipped to tackle that big pile of papers accumulating on your desk.

3. Plan to take a 'mental health day'. Some companies have incorporated this sanity-saver in annual leave entitlements, but a weekend day will do just as well. Go to a health farm,

spend the day in bed watching soppy videos or reading trashy romances, eat cookie dough or lounge around with a friend. Learning to unwind will help ease the stresses and demands of daily life. You've earned it. Enjoy it.

4. Eat well, exercise, look after yourself. It may be obvious, but it's easy to neglect your health when the demands start piling up. Besides, you don't want to be ill in bed when that one-time golden opportunity arises. Nor do you want to be coughing and sputtering all over the CEO.

5. You know what to do, but it's worth repeating: Cut down on take-aways and junk food. Eat fresh fruit and vegetables. Exercise. Cut down on alcohol. Give up smoking.

When the Going Gets Tough, the Tough Keep Going (and Going and Going and Going)

Whether you've just decided to make some major changes to your career or have already embarked on this exciting new path, expect setbacks, disappointments and frustrations. I don't mean to steal your thunder or rain on your parade, but even your dream job will occasionally turn into a nightmare. The secret to success is not to abandon your new aspirations at the first hint of trouble, but to face up to your obstacles and find solutions. And this will take motivation.

Motivation is *key* to achieving our goals. It's absolutely crucial. With motivation and drive you will stay committed to realizing your dreams. When motivation dwindles, it's as good as giving up. The challenge, therefore, is to look at strategies to help you develop and maintain motivation. And that means looking at your needs.

The humanist psychologist Maslow can help us here. According to his view we are all subject to two very different sets of motivational states that need to be satisfied in order for us to thrive. The first refers to our **physiological needs** which ensure our safety and physical and psychological survival: shelter, food, protection, self-esteem, love and affection, and belonging. The second set of motivational states promote a person's **self-actualization**, which helps us realize our full potential as individuals through creative and intellectual pursuits.

The hierarchical nature of Maslow's model means that the needs lower down on the diagram must first be satisfied before we can move on up to the higher needs. So you must first satisfy your needs for food and drink before you can think about your other needs. If you are trying to concentrate on this book when you are tired or hungry, you probably won't have much success. Therefore, in order for you to make the most of your life and achieve your goals, it is essential that you first take good care of yourself and look after your emotional and physical well-being.

Maslow discovered, however, that people who realize their full potential tend to share certain traits in common. If you think for a minute about examples of people in history who are true self-actualizers, I am sure you won't have too much trouble coming up with a few names, such as Martin Luther King, Eleanor Roosevelt, Albert Einstein, Gandhi, and many other politicians, leaders, sportsmen and -women and others whose lives were devoted to reaching their highest aspirations. Whether you aim to be president of the United States or president of the PTA, run a large company or run in the local marathon, travel the seven seas or visit a neighbouring city, they are all worthy goals for any self-actualizers.

Characteristics of Self-actualizers

1. *They can cope with uncertainty.*
2. *They accept themselves for who they are.*
3. *They are spontaneous thinkers and doers.*
4. *They focus on problems and tasks.*
5. *They have a good sense of humour.*
6. *They have an ability to evaluate life objectively.*
7. *They are very creative individuals.*
8. *They are not purposely unconventional, but are able to maintain their individuality.*
9. *They have a particular concern for humanity and the common good.*
10. *They are appreciative of just being alive and the life experience.*
11. *They establish deep, meaningful relationships with a few people.*

Take a few moments and think about the characteristics of self-actualizers. Now, I want you to come up with the name of a person, perhaps a friend of yours or maybe a role model from your community, or even a television personality whom you have never met. Just someone who has qualities that you admire. Someone you would describe as an achiever. In thinking about this person and his or her accomplishments and achievements, I want you to write down below all the qualities about that person that have made him or her a self-actualizer. What is it that has contributed to his or her success? Try to identify traits from the list above and also, if you want, come up with others of your own.

What Makes My Friend/Role Model a Self-actualizer?

1.
2.
3.
4.
5.
6.
7.
8.
9.
10.

Maslow's lesson to us is that it's essential for our own self-worth to achieve, to create, to feel.

Of course, there may be some important reasons why you stick with a job you hate. You have a huge mortgage. You are supporting a family. You like the lifestyle it affords you. These are all perfectly acceptable reasons for carrying on with your job. However, even in this scenario, if you want to feel more fulfilled as an individual and increase your chances of personal happiness and success, then you can always think about developing yourself in other ways. A hobby. Community service. Local politics. A degree.

Everyone has some talent or some interest that sets them apart from everyone else. In the space below I want you to start thinking about which of Maslow's self-actualizer traits you can use in order to help achieve your goal. In the second column, write down an example of a time when you exhibited this trait.

Maslow's Traits	My Traits
1.	1.
2.	2.
3.	3.
4.	4.
5.	5.
6.	6.
7.	7.
8.	8.
9.	9.
10.	10.

Top Tips for Success

Getting On with Workmates

1. In the office, listening skills are important. A good listener will take in information about other people and remember it. This will make others feel important.
2. Maintain friendly relationships with everyone, and don't become identified as part of a clique. Others will feel excluded.
3. Take your turn making the coffee and tea or bringing in the biscuits.
4. Even if you only have 5 minutes to grab lunch, take an extra 30 seconds and wash your plate, cup and utensils. They pile up very quickly, and dirty dishes are a major source of office friction.

I Think I Can, I Think I Can – Actually, I'm Not Too Sure: Challenging Self-doubts

In pursuing your dreams, there's one main requirement: Believing in yourself. Our beliefs about ourselves, other people and the world at large have a huge impact on our lives. They are usually subconscious and have the power to be either constructive or destructive. When disabling and disempowering, they act as a little voice in our heads telling us why we can't achieve the things we want out of life.

Many of our beliefs, both negative and positive, came from childhood, from our parents, teachers and other adult figures who helped shape our lives.

How many of the following sound familiar?

- *You never had a head for mathematics.*
- *You were always a spoiled child.*
- *Children should be seen and not heard.*
- *You will never amount to anything.*

- *Why can't you be more like your brother or sister?*
- *You were trouble from the moment you were born.*
- *You never think of anyone but yourself.*
- *You are stupid.*
- *You were always gifted in languages.*
- *It's a dog-eat-dog world. People cannot be trusted.*
- *Women are inferior.*
- *Ethnic minorities are lazy and stupid.*
- *Never trust anyone.*

This list is not exhaustive. No doubt some of these beliefs will resonate with you, while others won't.

Right now I just want you to think more about the many ways positive and negative beliefs impact your life. This process often takes a bit of time and a bit of patience, but before too long you will be able to identify those little voices in your head that help you and hinder you. Identifying these voices or beliefs is important, because they tend to act as self-fulfilling prophesies. In other words, if you believe you aren't capable of success, you're more likely to give up.

Kristina's Golden Rules for Success

If you were raised surrounded by negativity or have low self-esteem, don't despair. The good news is that you can develop your own belief system that will fill you with confidence and help keep you on track.

These are my rules for success. I know they work, because I live by them. What's more, they're easy to follow and will help do wonders for your personal life as well as your professional one.

1. *In order to reduce conflict, it's important to accept that every person is different.*
2. *People make decisions based on the evidence available at the time.*
3. *There is no such thing as failure, only feedback.*
4. *Every behaviour has a positive intention behind it.*
5. *The meaning of the communication can be seen in the response you get.*
6. *Every problem is solvable.*
7. *The most successful people are those who are flexible in their thinking strategies.*
8. *People who would rather have peace of mind than be right all the time are the happiest and most stress-free.*
9. *If at first you don't succeed, try a different approach.*
10. *The worst that can happen is you'll get a negative response.*
11. *There's no time like the present.*

Now let's take a look at each one in more detail.

In Order to Reduce Conflict, Accept that Every Person Is Different

This statement may seem like common sense, but don't dismiss it just yet. Everyone has their own view of the world, based on their own experiences. As a result, no one is necessarily right or wrong; people just have differing interpretations. Sometimes they'll match yours. Other times, they won't. However, once you accept that someone else's perspective is equally valid – even though you may not agree with their views – then you automatically understand, accept and tolerate these differences. Basically, this rule focuses on respecting someone else's right to their opinions.

> *Jo was wondering which career direction to go into. She always knew she had a talent for languages and thought she might like to live abroad for a while. Her parents thought taking time off after she completed her degree to live in France would be a waste of time. They wanted her to go to law school, which they insisted she should do as soon as she finished university. If she took a year off to go traipsing around the world, she'd probably never study law. And then what would she do for a career?*

This is the type of scenario that happens when someone doesn't acknowledge that everyone is different. Unfortunately, it is also very common. Jo's parents came from a different generation, a different time. Their emphasis on immediate professional success through a law qualification reflected their concerns and values. Jo's view was that she wanted to explore her other talents and learn a bit about the world around her before she settled into a career.

Accepting that other people perceive and interpret the world differently from you means you respect the differences, and this reduces conflict. Jo's parents had to learn to let go, let their daughter grow up, realize her independence and make her own mistakes. Jo has to learn that her parents will always worry about her and love her, and only have her career and best interests at heart, based on their own experiences.

People Make Decisions Based
on the Evidence Available at the Time

When we make disastrous decisions about our lives, we tend to reassess these mistakes based on time, distance and the outcome of the event. Then we chastize ourselves for our own incompetence or look for scapegoats, conveniently forgetting that we made the best decision we could at the time – no one sets out to make bad decisions.

This is also wide-reaching and pervasive.

Robert decided to set up his own business. He had been working for a management consulting firm for 15 years and had begun resenting his job. His boss was also unsupportive and demeaning; Robert had been passed over for promotion on a number of occasions. In general Robert liked the work, but found the long hours demanding and his colleagues competitive and unsupportive. Since Robert was becoming increasingly unhappy at work, one day he decided to quit the company and set up his own business in the same field. Both he and his wife discussed all the pros and cons and decided that the advantages out-weighed the disadvantages.

A year later, Robert and his wife weren't quite so optimistic. Although he had been very successful in many ways, Robert found that he was working even longer hours. He was responsible for seeking out clients, doing the actual work, keeping up with the admin, generating ideas on his own, etc. He found he was becoming increasingly more depressed and stressed and having difficulties coping with the pressures. Robert and his wife began arguing, because the demands of his new consultancy meant infrequent contact with his family. She resented having to be both mother and father to their children and was concerned about dwindling finances. He resented her lack of appreciation for the pressures he was facing.

After a year, Robert had had enough and began applying for jobs with different firms. Unfortunately he felt like a failure as a businessman and a family man, and his marriage is still recovering from the strain.

The problem here is that both Robert and his wife lost sight of the original reasons he decided to set up on his own in the first place, and were focusing too much on the outcome. Both of them acted on the information they had at the time, when it genuinely seemed that Robert would be better off going it alone in business.

There Is No Such Thing as Failure, Only Feedback

Because many people have aspirations and ambitions, they tend to think of success and failure in black-and-white terms. I truly believe that failure does not exist. We can learn something positive and useful from even the bleakest situations. However, when we make a bad decision we tend to blame ourselves for being incompetent. Our confidence dwindles and we stop trying. We feel defeated and foolish.

I've banished the word failure from my lexicon, and concentrate instead on what I can learn from the situation. In other words, I focus on the feedback. Not only do I avoid the threat to my confidence, but I learn from the experience with my confidence still intact. And, believe me, there've been plenty of self-esteem-challenging moments in my life.

> *I've always loved the theatre and decided to write a play, a comedy about hippy therapists called* Shrink Resistant. *I'm also pleased to say that a theatrical producer has offered to put on my play. While this turn of events is a success, I've only been able to achieve this goal through viewing failure as feedback. When I first sent out my play I received rejection letter after rejection letter, detailing all the reasons why my play was sub-standard. However, while the initial news was hurtful and the temptation was to consign the script to the bin and nurse my bruised ego, I instead took the advice of my rejectors and made the necessary amendments to my script. I'm now looking forward to opening night.*

Every Behaviour Has a Positive Intention Behind It

Many of us become disarmed by the negative reactions of others. However, by reframing every negative behaviour in a positive light, we can maintain control.

> *I used to work as a consultant for an advertising company and the CEO was a real bully. He used to take delight in humiliating and demeaning his employees in front of others. I worked with these employees – although it wasn't part of my remit – to help them regain their confidence and maintain their composure whenever the CEO felt the urge to bully.*

*My advice? I asked them to think of something positive
in the CEO's behaviour towards them. It wasn't so difficult –
in fact it was very easy. Some said the positive message was they
would never treat their employees that way, others comforted
themselves in the fact that they weren't as insecure as the CEO,
because only a person lacking in self-esteem would feel the
need to belittle others. Once they'd adopted these views, they
found themselves in a position of superiority and control.*

The Meaning of the Communication
Can Be Seen in the Response You Get

Have you ever been in a situation where you think you have
explained something 'till you are blue in the face' and still the
person hasn't got the message? Then you will have experienced
first-hand the true meaning of this phrase. The importance of
this belief is that you can gain control over the responses that
you get from others, with just a little bit of effort.

*Kevin worked as a management consultant for a large firm.
Because he thought of himself as thorough and efficient,
whenever he was stuck at solving a problem he would knock
on his boss' door seeking assistance. Because this man had
several more years' experience, Kevin just automatically
assumed his boss would help him – but this was not the case.
Whenever he asked his boss for advice, Kevin was surprised at
the impatient and irritated response he got.*

*I asked Kevin to do some 'homework'. I suggested that
although the obvious response when having difficulties solving*

a problem would be for him to turn to someone with more experience, maybe his boss had a different view. I asked him to look around at his colleagues and assess the reasons why his boss seemed to get along better with some than others. After a few days, Kevin realized why. His boss, a very busy man with an incredible workload of his own, did not want to take the time to 'hold someone's hand'. He preferred to guide and offer advice to employees who would present a problem and then offer possible solutions to that problem. They would then discuss the pros and cons of these solutions. When Kevin came to him for help, his boss believed that Kevin was really looking for someone else to do his job. When Kevin began offering possible solutions to the problems he faced, relations with his boss improved immediately.

Every Problem Is Solvable

How do you act when you are faced with a problem that needs solving? Do you give up easily, try many different methods and approaches to solve it, or do you leave it up to someone else to solve it for you? This 'golden rule' is all about believing that you *can* solve the problem by placing stock in your own creativity and developing lateral thinking. You just need to open up your mind to all the different possibilities and not get locked into one type of solution.

The Most Successful People Are Those Who Are Flexible in Their Thinking Strategies

In relationships or at work, flexibility is the best approach. The more choices and options you have available to you, the more you will be likely to succeed.

Gilbert worked as a manager for a computer sales company. Detail-orientated – in fact, very anally-retentive, Gilbert was very methodical and precise about his work. Most of the time Gilbert's careful approach was appropriate. Few mistakes were made and decisions were reached only after much thought. However, on a number of occasions Gilbert was passed over for promotion and he had no idea why. We discussed his work habits and his relationships with colleagues and it soon became obvious that, where Gilbert viewed himself as thorough, his workmates perceived him as rigid. Gilbert lacked flexibility. When deadlines were moved forward, Gilbert was unable to adapt his work habits, which put pressure on the rest of the team. He was unwilling to learn the new technology because he had already perfected the old. Gilbert was unable to see anyone else's point of view once he had come to a decision.

No doubt, Gilbert was very good at some aspects of his job, but his lack of flexibility and his tendency to plod along often grated with the other demands of the job, and this inflexibility was holding him back professionally and personally.

People Who Would Rather Have Peace of Mind than Be Right All the Time Are the Happiest and Most Stress-free

I have an aunt who is determined that she is right all the time. She will argue a point, even if it is wrong, just to save face. Once she even argued until she was blue in the face that Florida bordered Texas. Even when we pointed out to her that you had to drive through Alabama, Mississippi and Louisiana before you could get to Texas, she still refused to be convinced.

Everyone wants to save face, but it is not worth losing your relationships, your friends and even your pride over a silly argument or petty details.

If at First You Don't Succeed, Try a Different Approach

In our society there is a belief that the secret to success is not giving up, to keep pursuing your goals until you finally achieve them. I agree. To a point. However, if you keep banging your head against the wall over and over again, you're only going to end up with a sore head. Achieving success requires more than just effort; it means abandoning a strategy that's not working and trying something else.

Samuel wanted a career in television and sent off his CV to all kinds of production companies. Although he had no previous experience of working in the industry – Samuel had just graduated with a B.A. – he was prepared to take just about any entry-level job offered and was determined to work hard to move up the ladder. Unfortunately Samuel received one rejection letter after another and was just about to give up and apply for other jobs when he contacted me.

Samuel's tactic of sending out CVs was clearly not working. Upon looking at his CV, it was clearly OK but it wouldn't really grab someone's attention. And, since television is a very competitive career to get into, and because producers receive countless applications and resumes from people every day, Samuel's needed some work.

*My first piece of advice to Samuel was **not** to send out the same CV to every prospective employer, but to tailor the document to demonstrate Samuel was the kind of person who would benefit each specific company. Since Samuel was answering advertisements in newspapers, I suggested that he amend his CV to reflect the requirements specified in the ad. If they asked for someone energetic, motivated and hard-working, then his CV and cover letter **had** to demonstrate that he had these qualities.*

Our CV is our calling card and an important marketing and PR tool. If it's sloppy, full of spelling mistakes and inaccuracies, crumpled and late, then what message is that likely to deliver? Not a very impressive one.

Despite all this hard work on Samuel's CV, I had to break the bad news to him. Very few people get jobs through advertisements. Often employers already have someone in mind for a job, but have to advertise for legal reasons. The best way to get a job is through networking. Samuel claimed he knew no one who worked in television, but I asked him to ask his parents, their friends, and anyone else he could think of.

In the interim, I suggested he call up a local television station and find out if he could volunteer time, as an intern. Not only would this opportunity give Samuel valuable experience of working on site, something he could add to his CV and discuss during interviews, he would also be on the scene should a position open up. I know this from my own experience. I was given my first job in media broadcasting the news for a local radio station because the newsreader had the flu and there was no one else to do it. Because I was hanging around on a Sunday afternoon, filing records and doing other tedious jobs, and since no one else was there, the station was grateful that I saved the day.

With these new approaches in mind, Samuel landed a job in television in three months, being offered a position as researcher on the show he'd been making coffee for.

The Worst that Can Happen Is You'll Get a Negative Response

Making the necessary changes to achieve your goals can be intimidating and scary. Many people, even those with clear ambitions, become anxious about picking up the phone or approaching a potential boss or influential contact. Sometimes the anxieties are so great that people put off making the calls, and sometimes abandon their goals.

While I understand that venturing into the unknown is frightening, many people don't take the time to stop and think about the *cause* of their anxiety. They feel the fear and just want to avoid it. However, if you make a call or introduce yourself to an influential person, the absolute worst possible scenario is they will say no. Now, I know a negative response can be unpleasant, but it's not the end of the world. It's not even the final say. I refer you back to rule number three. If you don't get that job, call the personnel manager and find out why your qualifications weren't adequate. If you were passed over for promotion, make an appointment with your boss to learn why. Even the most negative of feedback will provide you with something positive that will improve your chances of achieving your goal.

1 There's No Time Like the Present

This rule refers to timing. Once you've formulated goals and outlined your plans for success, then get to it. Don't hang about. Don't wait for 'a more opportune moment'. There's no better time than *right now*. Of course, I'm not asking you to jack in your present job or invest all your money in a new venture. I am, however, encouraging you to go out and begin achieving your goals. NOW.

Matthew was a 32-year-old client of mine who was unhappy working as an accountant. When he was an undergraduate, Matthew had been attracted to the world of journalism, but his father had convinced him that accounting was a more stable career. After 10 years of working in this field, Matthew was beginning to feel more and more bored. The money was good and his future was secure, but Matthew's attention once again turned to journalism. Together we discussed what this move would entail, and Matthew voiced two main concerns. First, he was concerned that his age might be a deterrent, especially as he had no track record as a reporter. And second, Matthew had become accustomed to his good salary and didn't relish the idea of working at an entry-level wage.

With these concerns in mind I advised Matthew to think about writing on a freelance basis. With his experience in accounting, I suggested he contact the business editors of various newspapers to discuss potential article ideas. This way, Matthew could try out the world of journalism without giving up the security of his day job.

The more we discussed journalism, the more Matthew became excited and animated. He started reeling off ideas for articles, so I suggested he pick up the phone – right here, right now – and call some editors. Shock, horror. The colour drained from Matthew's face, but since he had the ideas and the motivation, why wait? What did he have to lose? After I picked him up off the floor, Matthew called one of the editors of a well-respected broadsheet and pitched his idea. The editor was receptive; he advised Matthew to write the article and send it in on spec. Matthew went home and spent the weekend working on the piece, and the editor was delighted with the result. After that, Matthew began writing articles on a regular basis.

Matthew had the expertise and ability to have a go in the competitive world of journalism. He just lacked confidence and needed a push in the right direction.

My golden rules for success have helped Matthew and many other clients, and they will help you, too. They will help you restructure the way you view yourself, your abilities and your beliefs about achieving success. So, as an experiment, I want you to try some of them out. Perhaps you need to make a call about a job you're interested in, or maybe you want to find out about a degree course you're interested in. Go ahead. By adopting these rules you will find out that you have nothing to lose and absolutely everything to gain.

Top Tips for Success

All Work and No Play ... Life's Far Too Short!

1. A life dedicated to work may be rewarding, but where's the fun? Go out and enjoy the fruits of your labour.

2. If you've got it, flaunt it. Wear that daring new dress, the one that makes you feel sexy, feminine, attractive, confident and clings in all the right places.

3. Practise flirting and smiling. You're dressed up. You look gorgeous. So go out and mingle.

4. There may be safety in numbers, but avoid travelling in a pack. You'll seem less approachable if you're surrounded by an entourage.

5. Go somewhere new. Grab a friend and go to Prague for the weekend, or take up skiing. Too adventurous? Then how about an exotic restaurant, dance club or sophisticated wine bar? Breaking free from your routine will be exciting. Who knows what might happen?

Success and Setbacks:
The Challenge Is Yours

Some days, everything you touch will turn to gold. Other days you'll wonder why you even got out of bed that morning. It's easy to take responsibility when things are going our way and tempting to blame others when disaster strikes. In an ideal world all our plans would go like clockwork. But this is not an ideal world. On your path to success you will find the rough as well as the smooth. Are you willing to be fully accountable for all your decisions?

Successful people accept responsibility for their actions, decisions and mistakes. And so must you. There's no passing the buck. You're accountable for the lot. And I mean the lot. The good, the bad and the ugly. If you tend to shirk from responsibility, you won't be able to stay on top of things when obstacles arise.

Do you have what it takes? Answer the following questions and find out.

- *Do you blame yourself for past mistakes?*
- *Do you leave things to chance?*
- *Do you lack judgement?*
- *Do you dislike taking charge of a situation?*
- *Do you have problems sticking to decisions once you've made them?*
- *Do you frequently compare your situation to that of others?*

If you've answered yes to these questions, then you probably tend to point your fingers in someone else's direction when disaster strikes. If so, to you, accepting responsibility has negative connotations. But nothing could be further from the truth. Being accountable means becoming informed, remaining committed to your goals, having the courage to take risks and learning from your mistakes. It's proactive and positive.

With these thoughts in mind, I want you to try the following exercise. The aim is to show you how easy it is to transform any situation in which you have felt victimized to one of empowerment and control.

I want you to think of a few situations, maybe three or four, in your life when you felt you weren't in control, that someone had taken advantage of you. Perhaps a work colleague passed your ideas off as his own. Or maybe a close friend betrayed a confidence. Maybe someone toyed with your emotions.

1.

2.

3.

4.

Now I would like you to imagine you are facing the person who disappointed you, and telling them:

'You did this to me [whatever the situation was] and you made me feel this way [whatever your reaction was]'.

Once you have written this down, I want you to concentrate on how you felt. In each situation you probably felt hurt, angry, maybe bitter, rejected, foolish, depressed, unconfident, and most likely a great many other negative emotions. These negative emotions are destructive because they make us feel victimized and lacking in control.

Now I want you to go back to each of these scenarios and think about them in a new way:

'I placed myself [in this situation] in which the outcome was unpleasant and I made myself feel [your reaction]'.

The difference might at first be a subtle one. But the more you begin thinking about situations – even disastrous ones – from a position of control and empowerment, the more you will feel in a position of control. You will still most likely feel disappointed or betrayed, but when you take responsibility for all aspects of your life, you gain options. You are now in a better position to deal with situations so that you minimize the risk of their happening again. If someone stole your ideas, you now know, for example, to keep records of meetings, to make it known in all kinds of ways to your boss that you are the creative force behind a given project. You can also prepare yourself with a ready-made reason for not working with that person again. In other words, forewarned is forearmed. You are no longer a victim, you are now in charge.

Taking Care of Business Means Looking after Your Health

Whether you choose to set up on your own or plan to shoot up the corporate ladder, it's essential that you look after your health. Many of us take our health for granted, but your career will go nowhere if you're taking time off because you're ill. The powers that be won't be impressed if you're not around when they need you. Your business won't run itself if you're in bed with a fever.

Success in your chosen career will mean taking extra care of your health. I can't underscore this enough. You will have to eat well, make time for exercise and develop strategies to handle stress.

Working Hard and Hardly Working?

Do you constantly feel that the demands in your life far outstrip your energy supply? Are you always letting family and friends down because your time is so limited? Do you feel guilty when you take time to relax? Do you have problems winding down at the end of a busy day?

If so, no wonder you're exhausted and burnt out. Where's the joy in living? Where's the fulfilment? In our society, we value hard work. If you're like many high-fliers, you no doubt equate your self-worth with your career. But pushing yourself and working till you drop is not the answer. It is possible to accomplish your goals and invest your energies without damaging your health.

LAUREN AND TONY: THE MODERN COUPLE

Lauren was a 31-year-old management consultant. Both she and her husband, Tony, who also worked in the same profession, spent more time travelling on business than with each other. Mondays through Wednesdays, Lauren was working in the Prague office, while Tony was off in Singapore during the rest of the week. They often had to work on weekends as well, and when they weren't catching up on paperwork, Lauren and Tony were more likely catching up on their sleep.

For several years they both thrived on the hectic pace of their schedules. They loved the variety. They got a buzz from the travel. The money they earned afforded them a beautiful home and expensive cars. They were both very clearly dedicated to their careers, and their hard work was rewarded by frequent bonuses and promotions. Then, one day, Lauren came to me. She was concerned because she had been passed over for a job she'd assumed she'd get. All of sudden, she began to question her dedication and felt insecure about her career.

When I began working with Lauren, she informed me that all her energies and activities centred around work. And, although she loved and respected her husband, Lauren felt that they were both beginning to feel the strain of their demanding workload. To me, it was obvious that Lauren (if not Tony as well) needed to simplify her life. If she carried on working at this pace, I was concerned she might collapse.

So, we decided a little spring cleaning was in order. The first thing Lauren decided to do was to hire a cleaner for their house. Amazingly, Lauren and Tony shared the chores on weekends – somehow they just never quite got around to hiring a cleaning service – but due to other demands, the housework never quite got finished and there was clutter everywhere. In spring-cleaning her house, Lauren was able to see the benefits of uncluttering the rest of her life. With her home better organized, Lauren also began to feel she had more control over her life. She had hated coming home to a messy house. It used to depress her and make her feel guilty.

Next, we discussed ways of boosting her physical and mental health. As a teenager, Lauren had been a keen runner and had even entered a few marathons. Not only had she enjoyed competitive running, but she had found the activity, the fresh air, the time on her own had produced therapeutic benefits. In fact, she used to joke that running kept her sane *and without the exercise she'd have to resort to therapy! Lauren decided to go running every morning before work, and would use the time to prioritize her day. Even with these few changes, Lauren already began to feel more in control of her life. She felt more energized and started to think more proactively about her career.*

We next focused on her relationship with her husband. With their impossible schedules, time was obviously a precious and rare commodity. Even though the opportunities were limited, Lauren discovered that she and Tony could spend Wednesday and Saturday nights together. They both agreed that they would spend this time promoting intimacy and closeness. They decided they wouldn't speak about work or other obligations, and just relax in each other's company.

We then examined Lauren's work situation and explored some of the reasons for her recent insecurities. She realized that the sacking of a close colleague had left her feeling threatened. She began avoiding her boss, the man who'd fired her friend, because she didn't want to end up on the chopping block. But, while her strategy of avoidance was helping her feel more secure in the short term, it was also producing more profound fears and insecurities. So, instead of hiding from her boss, I suggested to Lauren that she increase her contact with him. This man was important for her career and Lauren needed to build a solid relationship with him.

In taking the initiative to increase her contact with her boss, Lauren realized that she enjoyed working with him. She liked his ideas and began working on joint projects with him. Within three months, Lauren's profile in the company had increased. She was now perceived as a visionary and her hard work was being acknowledged by her entire department. She was thrilled. Lauren began to take on more responsibility, manage bigger projects and develop more of a leadership role. There's no stopping her now!

De-Stress for Success

Lauren and Tony are no different from many modern couples, trying to juggle the demands of competitive, busy careers and a home life. In learning how to handle stress and explore the problem areas in their lives, they both became healthier, happier and more focused

Most of us also have first-hand experience of stress. It is part and parcel of modern life and, unfortunately, unavoidable. When we feel the effects of stress, we are not coping well with the demands in our lives.

While the harmful effects of stress are well documented, it may surprise you to know that some stress is actually good for you. Stress actually motivates us to get out of bed in the morning, to get to work, to go to school, to achieve something in our lives. Without some stress, in fact, we wouldn't be able to function at all.

The Harmful Effects of Stress

However, too much stress in our lives is dangerous to our health. When you feel your life is spiralling out of control and you feel powerless to cope with all the mounting pressures, your stress levels are likely to be harmful. This is not uncommon. Stress-related health problems, like asthma, ulcers, diabetes, dizziness, depression, nausea, indigestion, a racing pulse, trembling, rheumatoid arthritis, hypertension and, most seriously of all, heart disease, stroke and even cancer, are just some of the many harmful ways that stress takes its toll on our health. It can lead to death. In fact, doctors now tell us that the number of stress-related deaths has reached epidemic proportions. Furthermore, stress costs millions, if not billions, in absenteeism from work.

Recent studies have even shown that too much stress shrinks our brains!

Identifying Stress in Your Life

In order to reduce the sources of stress in your life, you first need to identify them. Generally we feel the symptoms of stress, or distress, when we feel frustrated, pressurized, prevented from achieving a goal or when we face conflict – these seem to be the main sources of stress.

How Do You Experience Stress?

1. *Are you irritable and short-tempered about small things that would not normally bother you?*
   YES/NO

2. *Do you find you are no longer interested in work-related and other activities that you once found fascinating?*
   YES/NO

3. *Are you feeling excessively tired?*
   YES/NO

4. *Do you find that you have to make excuses for not attending meetings, or getting work done on time, or not working to your normal level?*
   YES/NO

If you answered yes to all or most of these questions, then you should begin analysing your life to see if stress is causing you to behave differently from normal. One way of doing this is to calculate the number of stressors in your life. Look below at the following list and note the many different sources of stress:

Sources of Stress

The Social Readjustment Scale (Holmes and Rahe 1967)

Life Event Score

Death of a spouse	100
Divorce	73
Marital separation	65
Gaol term	63
Death in the family	63
Injury or illness	53
Marriage	50

Job loss	47
Retirement	45
Marital reunion	45
Family illness	44
Pregnancy	40
Sexual problems	39
New family member	39
Business problems	39
Change in economic status	38
Death of a friend	37
New job	36
Increased marital conflict	35
Mortgage	31
Mortgage foreclosure	30
Change in work duties	29
Children leaving home	29
In-law difficulties	29
Personal success	28
Partner gets new or loses old job	26
Starting or completing school	26
Change in the way you live	25
Review of personal habits	24
Problems with work supervisor	23
Change in number of work hours	20
Moving house	20
Change of hobbies	20
Change in church routine	20
Change in socializing	18
Loan for small purchase	17
Change to sleep patterns	16

Change in number of family reunions   15

Change in diet or eating patterns   15

Vacation time   13

Christmas holidays   12

Minor infractions of the law   11

Major stressful changes and events often tend to overshadow the more minor hassles of everyday life, but they too can cause stress and distress. So, be aware of them. Although they are not quite as disruptive or as dramatic, the minor everyday hassles can also lead to stress.

Throughout the day people can suffer from a variety of different hassles: being late for work, missing the bus, losing one's keys, going to the bank only to find a long queue, having to deal with rude people like customers or bank tellers. These minor hassles can also affect your physical health, causing headaches, the flu and sore throats.

Coping with Stress

Identifying the stressors in your life is the first step to reducing or even eliminating their harmful effects. But you also need to learn to cope with stress. Many people compound the ill-effects of stress by not seeking help. Some people think that they are weak or incompetent because they are having difficulty coping with stress, but nothing could be further from the truth. Facing up to the problems in your life is the sign of someone who is capable, efficient and in control. By not addressing the problems of stress, the physical and emotional symptoms are only likely to get worse – leading to depression and a nervous breakdown.

How Do You Cope with the Stressful Events in Your Life?

When faced with stressful events, do you bury your head in the sand? Hide underneath the covers? Ignore the problems in the fervent hope that they will disappear all by themselves?

Wrong approach. Problems very rarely, if ever, go away by themselves. In fact, if you don't face up to your sources of stress and your problems, they will only become worse.

Some people seek comfort through alcohol, shopping, excessive exercise, overeating – in fact, any activity that keeps their mind busy on something else.

Again, wrong approach. These 'treats' may provide us temporary relief and comfort by blocking our problems, but in the long run they only provide us with a short-term escape. So, 3,000 calories or a few hundred pounds later, your problems will still be there.

Do you blame other people or your situation for your troubles?

Guess what? Wrong response again. Surrendering all responsibility for your problems to someone else or to another situation means giving in and giving up. As you know by now, being a victim is not a healthy response and will only make you feel helpless in the face of your problems. Feeling that you are in control, that you are able to make positive changes to your advantage, is the way to get results.

Healthy Ways to Handle Stress

Right now, I want you to take a few moments and think about a particularly stressful situation that you are currently facing. If you can't think of one that is troubling you at the moment, try to come up with one from your past. Get a piece of paper and describe the situation.

No doubt, in thinking about this stressful situation, you are beginning to feel a bit bad, perhaps anxious. So many of the negative emotions associated with stress, however, are due to the fact that people are failing to find a practical solution for their problems. Once you face up to the stress and resolve it, all the negativity should disappear.

Now, even through your stress I want you to begin thinking about how you can resolve the problem, or even part of the problem. You can even brainstorm ideas: for this, take about 60 seconds to list a whole range of possible solutions to your problem, no matter how far-fetched or absurd they may seem. Alternatively, you can address a small aspect of the problem itself. Facing a huge problem can be intimidating and stressful. However, breaking the problem down into manageable components aids tremendously in finding a solution.

Suppose, for example, you are having great difficulty keeping up with the demands of your job. You are swamped by the amount of work you have to do. You get ahead, only to find out that you are really weeks behind. This is a common enough problem for many of us. Feeling overwhelmed by an enormous task can alone de-motivate us and make us feel powerless.

The first strategy you can adopt would be to assess the workload itself realistically. Is your workload unrealistic, given your job expectations and salary? Or are you just not getting down to the tasks – arriving late to work, gossiping with co-workers, letting your personal problems distract you during office hours?

If you firmly believe your workload is too demanding, then maybe you should try having a discussion with your boss. However, if he or she thinks you should be able to keep up, then you may risk losing confidence (your boss' and your own!) in your abilities.

If you need to catch up, the next thing you can do is to devote some more time out of office hours. This solution does not have to be permanent or even too drastic. You could work through lunch, come in an hour earlier or stay an hour later, or take work home on weekends. By devoting even a little bit more time to completing the tasks, you'll find you'll get a lot done.

Just by coming up with some practical solutions to help solve the problem will empower you to deal more effectively in stressful situations. Here are a few more guidelines:

1. *Physical exercise reduces tension. Providing you don't overdo it, physical exercise is a great way for dealing with stress.*

2. *Spending time with your friends and family and other people you like relaxes you by allowing you to laugh and enjoy yourself.*

3. *Planning things is also important. Having something that you look forward to doing is a great mood-elevator and will help get you through even the most stressful moments.*

4. *Know when to slow down. Don't allow yourself to become overstressed and ill. Begin to identify your symptoms of stress and learn to recognize what your stress threshhold is. For some people it's sleepless nights, for others it's headaches, for*

*others it is a racing pulse. Whatever the symptoms are that
signal to you that you are overdoing it, learn them, then slow
down.*

5. *Relaxation exercises. Learning to relax and to keep calm is
the most effective way of combating stress and, you know
what? You will feel terrific for your efforts – calm, in control,
tranquil. I cannot recommend enough the beneficial effects
of relaxation exercises. You might want to take up
meditation or learn auto-hypnosis, or buy a relaxation tape.
Whichever method you choose, you will achieve the same
important benefits.*

Top Tips for Success

Facing the University Challenge

Many people are flocking to higher education to improve their
career prospects. Even if you haven't set foot inside a classroom
in years, there's no need to feel anxious or overwhelmed. While
juggling the demands of work, home and studies won't be easy,
here are some top tips to see you through.

1. Find out ahead of time the requirements for your degree.
   Ask the admissions office about exams, dissertations,
   projects, attendance and the standards required. That way,
   you'll be fully informed about what's expected of you.
2. There's no such thing as a dumb question, so if you find
   yourself in the dark, don't be afraid to ask for clarification.

Trust me, if you're confused, most of the others will be as well.

3. Form a study group. This is a great way to share notes, offer support and improve your social life.

4. Attend all lectures and take detailed notes.

5. Make sure you meet all deadlines. Asking for extensions can lead to all kinds of stress and your work may be penalized.

6. Keep up with latest advances in library technology, including the library computer catalogues and CD-Roms. There's no room for techno-phobes, not even in the ivory tower.

7. Allow yourself plenty of time for exam revision. Putting it off until the last minute will only make you panic. You won't be able to concentrate or take in the information.

8. If you do find yourself following behind in work, **immediately** inform your course tutor and work out a solution. Even in a week or two, assignments can pile up and you will quickly feel swamped.

Putting It All Together: Your Goal Plan

You've completed the exercises. You've thought about your life, your dreams, the careers you find desirable and the ones you wouldn't want to touch with a barge pole. Now that the reflection phase is finished, it's time to think about specifying and formulating your goals. This step is very important. Studies have shown that the most successful people identify their goals and devise strategies to achieve them.

Have You Defined Your Goals?

If we were to ask most people what they would like to achieve out of life, success, retiring at 40, becoming a millionaire or achieving fame would no doubt be the most popular responses. The trouble is, though, these aren't goals; they're sentiments. Because these ambitions are vaguely worded there is no clear blueprint to follow. The first task in formulating your goals is to *be specific*. If you want to be a success, you have to specify the career that will help you achieve the wider aim. Teacher? Lawyer? Television presenter? In clearly defining your objective, you'll also have a better idea about how to pursue it.

Are Your Goals Realistic?

Once you've clearly specified your goal, you'll then have to determine if it's realistic. If it's not, you'll only end up feeling frustrated and disappointed. If you're in your mid-forties and your goal is to improve your tennis game, that's fine. However, if your aim is to beat Pete Sampras at Wimbledon, then your aspirations are too high. If, however, you've worked in an industry for 20 years and are thinking of setting up on your own, then your aims are more feasible.

One way of determining if your goals are realistic is to ask yourself the following questions:

- *Are my goals conceivable?*
- *Are my goals believable?*
- *Are my goals achievable?*

If you've answered yes to all these questions, then it sounds like your goals are realistic and feasible. If, however, your responses tended to lean in the negative direction, then it's time to have a rethink. I don't mean to be a damp squib or to pour water all over your dreams. After all, there are lots of examples of people who've reached the top against amazing odds. Margaret Thatcher never thought she'd see a woman prime minister in her lifetime. Sophie Dahl might be voluptuous in the extreme, but that didn't stop her from becoming one of the queens of the catwalk. Abraham Lincoln and Colonel Sanders only found success in their respective careers late in life. I firmly believe that anything is possible, but it doesn't hurt to take a reality check either.

Have You Identified Short-term and Long-term Goals?

There's a strong likelihood that you might have a number of goals you'd like to achieve. Some will probably be more immediate aims, while others will reflect long-term ambitions.

To help distinguish between your different objectives, the next step is to make a list of all the various personal and professional goals you'd like to achieve.

Professional Goals

In six months' time, I'd like to have achieved the following goals:

Within the next year, I'd like to achieve the following goals:

In the next three years, I'd like to achieve the following goals:

In the next five years, I'd like to achieve the following goals:

Over the next ten years, I'd like to achieve the following goals:

Personal Goals

In six months' time, I'd like to have achieved the following goals:

Within the next year, I'd like to achieve the following goals:

In the next three years, I'd like to achieve the following goals:

In the next five years, I'd like to achieve the following goals:

In the next ten years, I'd like to achieve the following goals:

Have You Got the Resources to Achieve Your Goals?

You will need to draw on a wide variety of resources in order to achieve your goals. Your talents, skills, sense of humour, intelligence, style, ability to relate well to people, health, stamina and commitment to putting in long hours are just some of the many resources you will need to draw on.

Which resources do you have? Which do you lack? Don't be too confident or self-deprecating. It's important that you're honest with yourself. By candidly appraising your skills and abilities, you can save yourself a lot of frustration and time. Having said this, training, dedication, commitment and just plain hard work are often the only resources you'll need to achieve success in your chosen field.

How Will You Know You've Achieved Your Goals?

In formulating your goals and setting out to achieve them, you'll also have to measure your success. Otherwise, how will you know you've achieved your aims? Some people use tangible measures such as money, possessions, position or job title as a barometer of their success, while others adopt more intangible gauges such as personal growth or experience. Understanding when a goal is completed is important, so that you can formulate and achieve new ambitions.

How Will Your Goals Change Your Life?

Whether you're single or married with family commitments, your goals will not exist in isolation. Other factors will have to be taken into account and you will need to analyse your goals in the wider context of your life. How will your family and friends be affected by your new ambitions? Will they have to make sacrifices? Will they be supportive of the inevitable changes, which may include moving house, financial constraints, adapting to your long working hours and all the other added stresses and pressures?

Will you feel you're missing out on a social life or neglecting your hobbies and interests? By analysing the full impact of your goals and aspirations on your life and those around you, you can anticipate difficulties and think about possible solutions. Maybe you'll find that you'll need to schedule a weekly 'family night' or pursue your goals at a slower pace, or take in a lodger to help with expenses. Everyone's situation will be unique; just remember that while you're making changes and pursuing new ambitions, those nearest and dearest to you will also be affected.

Goal Plan Worksheet

The main goals I want to achieve are:

The most important reason I want to achieve these goals are:

The steps I plan to take in achieving these goals are:

The ways other people can help me are:

Person/Possible ways he or she can help:

I will know my goals are being achieved if:

Some things that could interfere with my goals are:

Top Tips for Success

CV Solutions

CLIENT CONCERN

'I'm trying to put together a CV after having been made redundant. The problem is I've had a number of jobs during the past 10 years or so, because I would work for a company, save up some money and go travelling. Now I'm ready to settle down for more permanent employment, but my job history looks unfocused and lacks direction. It's a disaster. Please help.'

MY SOLUTION

The situation's far from hopeless. Make a list of all the jobs you've had and highlight what you've contributed to each company and the skills you learned. Travelling around the world also takes initiative, problem-solving skills, flexibility, the ability to communicate, adapting quickly to new situations and many other skills we need to use in the office place. A CV which highlights your successes as a freelancer or consultant, who is now offering

her services on a more permanent basis, should impress potential employers and detract attention from any 'holes' in your resume.

Part 2

Social
Intelligence
and the
Art of
Impressing
Others

Successful Networking

Now that you have identified your goals, it's time to go out and pursue them. No doubt you already have some idea of how to go about achieving your ambitions. If you want to become a captain of industry, some experience in your chosen field and a Master's Degree in Business may be the way forward for you. If your dream is to spend a year in South America, then you've probably paid a visit to a local travel agency and thought about brushing up on your Spanish. If your ambition is to write the definitive novel of your generation, then you've probably checked out creative writing courses.

In planning and pursuing your dreams, I'm sure you've already thought about the time and energy you'll need and the sacrifices you'll need to make. And you're right. Achieving goals will require effort and hard work on your part. However, no man (or woman) is an island and you'll find your goals easier to achieve if you seek out the help of others. That means making contacts and networking.

How do you feel about relying on other people to help you achieve what you want? Uncomfortable? Ill at ease? You are not alone. There is a strong and enduring myth in our society that our achievements are only valid and worthwhile if we accomplish them on our own. If we show signs of any struggle along the way or, God forbid, have to seek someone else's advice or guidance, then the rewards are, well, not so rewarding.

Take a look at your own attitudes towards success. Do you feel you always have to do it alone? Be the expert? Be in total control?

Make no mistake. Accomplishing what we want out of life requires hard work, dedication and drive. But very rarely do we actually achieve our goals exclusively on our own. Our best athletes wouldn't be breaking the records and collecting their medals without the support of coaches, trainers and sponsors. Our impressive exam achievements may not be so glowing without the help of lecturers, seminars, study groups and the sympathetic friend who brings us coffee and cheers us on when we've convinced ourselves in a panic that we're going to fail. Or what about the family friend who knows someone, who knows someone else, who has an acquaintance, who just might have a job going?

I'm not trying to undermine your achievements, but I just want to point out that if we're all really, truly honest with ourselves, most of us have received some support from others along the way. Still not entirely convinced? Before we go on, maybe we should look at your fears or concerns about networking. Take a minute to write down on a separate piece of paper your negative thoughts about receiving support from others.

Now, take a look at the following list. How many match what you've put on your own list?

- *I don't like the idea of using people.*
- *I don't want to be obligated to others.*
- *I'm afraid of rejection.*
- *If I ask for help, I'll seem pushy.*
- *People might think I'm incapable.*
- *I don't have the energy or the time for the effort involved.*
- *People who network are ruthless and pretentious go-getters.*

All of these concerns are very common, but unfounded. Networking and relying on contacts is not a sign of weakness or inadequacy on your part. Far from it. Nor, of course, is it a ticket to exploit others for your own personal gain. Successful networking is a co-operative endeavour, not a competitive one. It's not about relying on others, but about give and take. It's about developing mutual relationships with people, and it's worth the time commitment on your part. You may be more than capable of achieving your goals on your own, but why make the task unnecessarily hard? Developing networking skills will not only create new opportunities for you, but new relationships as well.

How Networking Can Help You

Now that you've addressed your fears, think now about all the positive ways that networking benefits you. Here are some of the many reasons why two (or more!) heads can be better than one:

- *the opportunity to share ideas, contacts, skills and information*
- *a great way to develop team-building and a positive work environment*
- *the process is flexible and can be accomplished through phone calls, letters, faxes, lectures, seminars, conferences, meetings and newsletters*
- *other people can be a sounding board and provide constructive criticism*
- *professional and personal support.*

There are all kinds of benefits to networking, irrespective of your goals or your chosen field. Identifying your goals and willingness to dedicate your energy, time, resources and efforts to this plan are requirements that you alone can fulfil. Once you've made this commitment to yourself and your goals, sharing resources with others will not only help promote your success, but will be a more enjoyable process along the way. So, your task now is to contact a professional organization related to your chosen field. Your local council offices/chamber of commerce and library are good places to start.

Networking and building contacts reflect a process I call **social intelligence**, as discussed in the Introduction to this book. Simply put, social intelligence refers to a wide range of strategies you can adopt to impress people who may be influential in helping you achieve your goals. Networking is but one of many such skills. Over the remaining chapters in this book, we'll take a look at some of the others.

Top Tips for Success

Learning to Be a Nay-sayer: When Negativity Rules

Saying no to others is an essential, but tricky skill. Many times people cave in and say yes because they don't want to offend someone or come across as 'difficult'. But look what happens: If you always say yes, you'll soon be swamped with requests. You don't want to be a doormat, do you?

Learning to say no is all about self-preservation. If done properly, you won't offend anyone, but you will gain their respect. Here's how:

1. Only you can decide for yourself what is acceptable for you to take on. Sharing work is a great way of building rapport with colleagues. However, if you're pressed for time or the deal's not mutual, then enough's enough.
2. Once you've established your boundaries, don't budge for anyone.
3. Be calm and professional, but explain that you are not in a position to help. There's no need to elaborate. In fact, giving excuses will only encourage the other person to argue with you and wear you down.
6. If possible, offer them an alternative solution such as 'I could have helped if you'd given me more notice.'

Making Yourself Heard: Learning Assertiveness

Hannah was a client of mine. She came to see me for help. Hannah was stressed because she felt her work colleagues dismissed her views and failed to give her the respect she deserved. After meeting with Hannah a few times, I found out something interesting about her. She said she always had great difficulty expressing how she truly felt. Hannah was raised never to complain or express negative emotions. So, as a result, she became a timid and reticent person.

Hannah found interpersonal relationships difficult, particularly at work. Unfortunately, the ramifications of her lack of assertiveness were upsetting. Hannah wasn't able to delegate work assignments effectively because her colleagues had little respect for her. Because she felt uncomfortable expressing her annoyance, she tended to adopt an 'oh well, never mind' approach to things. Needless to say, she was becoming a doormat and her inability to assert herself was having an impact on her job.

In our discussions, we discovered that Hannah had a particular problem expressing anger, because she had come from a violent home. Once she understood the difference between anger (a healthy emotion) and aggression (a destructive behaviour), I gave her an assignment for the following week. I asked Hannah to allow herself to feel anger and to express it in a healthy way.

When I first made this suggestion to her, Hannah was of course shocked. Anger was something she was never allowed to feel, let alone express. So, when I gave her permission to be angry and to express it, she was understandably wary and nervous. One day during the week, Hannah was feeling particularly overworked, but had planned to leave the office on time due to plans she had made with her daughter. One of her colleagues wasn't able to finish a report due the following day, and assumed Hannah would stay late and work on it. Normally that was her practice, but not today. Not any more. Hannah explained to her workmate that she was unable to stay at the office and stated that the report was his responsibility, not hers. Much to her amazement, her colleague apologized and promised to stay in the office until the task was completed.

Something clicked for this woman. Once Hannah realized that she had the power to say no, she could then see she had been shouldering the burden of her department for far too long. Is it any wonder she was stressed? Being assertive and establishing new boundaries meant that Hannah was no longer being taken advantage of. She no longer dreaded going to work and felt her relationships with her colleagues had improved dramatically.

Hannah had learned the importance of **assertiveness**. Standing up for ourselves is not always easy. Most people want to be liked, to fit in, and they find the idea of confrontation distasteful. However, whether you want to work your way up the corporate ladder or branch out on your own, you will have to learn the skills of assertiveness.

Assertiveness Defined

Assertiveness means that you have the right to decide your own actions in a given situation, instead of automatically deferring to someone else or their demands. Being assertive also means recognizing and respecting the rights of other people.

Assertiveness has a bad reputation. People often feel uncomfortable about asserting what they want, either because they mistakenly equate assertiveness with pushiness or aggression or they believe it's impolite to ask for what you want. Assertiveness is actually a very positive quality and an important skill to develop. When you are using effective assertiveness skills you will come across as confident, calm, professional, direct and in control.

Your Rights as an Individual

1. *You have the right to express your opinions.*
2. *You have the right to tell others how you feel.*
3. *You have the right to ask others to change their behaviours and actions when they directly affect you.*

4. *You have the right to accept or reject what other people say to or request of you.*

Developing Assertiveness Skills

Developing assertiveness will be essential to your success, but it will take practice and require the skill of diplomacy. Remember, if nothing else, assertiveness is all about people-management. It's a fine juggling act between your needs and the egos of others.

If you are reticent or if the idea of expressing what you want from others fills you with dread, don't despair. There are lots of techniques that will help you improve your assertiveness skills. They are effective and will not only improve your assertiveness, but will help build your confidence in dealing with others.

COMMON SITUATIONS REQUIRING ASSERTIVENESS

*   *When you need to express how you are feeling.*
*   *When you need to share what you want or don't want.*
*   *When you need to convey what you're willing to do or not do for someone else.*
*   *When you need to inform someone else what you'd like them to do or not do.*

Broken Record Technique

The first strategy for building assertiveness is called the **broken record technique**. It's effective and easy to adopt.

Basically, while remaining very calm all you need do is to repeat over and over again why it's appropriate that you should be doing or not doing something – without excuses or arguments. Here's how:

> David: *Barbara, would you mind working late tonight and writing up this report for tomorrow?*
>
> Barbara: *I'd really like to help, but I can't work late tonight. I've got another commitment.*
>
> David: *This report really needs to be finished by tomorrow. The clients have been calling me all day asking for it.*
>
> Barbara: *I can appreciate the report is urgent, but I am unable to work late.*
>
> David: *It's not a lot of work. You can probably get it done in an hour or two.*
>
> Barbara: *That may be, but I've already arranged this other commitment.*
>
> David: *Can't you do me this one favour? I really need to get this report done.*
>
> Barbara: *I can see that you're in a difficult situation and I sympathize, but unfortunately, I've already arranged this other commitment.*

Simple, isn't it? Just by repeating a single phrase in response to the pleas of someone else, you're more likely to stand firm.

Fogging

The broken record technique works wonders in most situations, but at certain times, other methods will be more appropriate. That's when **fogging** will be helpful.

Many of my clients have complained that they occasionally get the blame at work for something they didn't do. Fogging is an excellent technique that can help defuse a situation which has the potential to be unpleasant or aggressive. Basically, the fogging technique smooths things over by suggesting that the person who is criticizing you may be partly right, even when you are convinced that they are wrong. Although this may seem like unassertive behaviour, it's not. When someone is angry, she or he *will not* be receptive to excuses. In fact, you will be perceived as defensive. The best approach, therefore, is to acknowledge what the person had to say and then change the direction of the conversation. Here's an example of fogging in action:

Boss: *You were supposed to bring the flip charts. How could you be so incompetent? You know how important they are to this presentation.*

Employee: *Maybe you're right. I should have made sure that someone brought the flip charts along.*

Boss: *Mistakes like this cost us business. Clearly, you can't be trusted with something as simple as that.*

Employee: *You're right, I still have a lot to learn when it comes to pitching to new clients.*

Boss: *See that it doesn't happen again and I'll overlook it this time.*

Employee: *It won't happen again.*

SITUATIONS IN WHICH FOGGING SHOULD BE USED

- *When you feel upset and are too emotional to discuss the matter calmly.*
- *When you're being insulted by a boss or colleague.*
- *When you're being unfairly criticized.*
- *When you are being criticized in front of colleagues or in a public forum.*
- *When you need some time-out, to calm down and collect your thoughts before you proceed.*

Negative Assertion

Fogging is an ideal technique to use in situations in which you feel you're being unfairly blamed, but there are times when you may be criticized for situations for which you might be accountable. **Negative assertion** is the best strategy to use in these circumstances. It will help defuse a potentially awkward situation and promote a more positive impression. Here's how it works:

Boss: *Look at your desk. It's a mess. It looks disorganized and sloppy. What does that say about your work habits?*
Employee: *Yes, it could use some straightening up.*
Boss: *Everyone else in the office manages to keep their desk tidy.*
Employee: *It is very cluttered, I agree.*
Boss: *We have certain expectations about orderliness.*
Employee: *I can see I need to be more organized and I'll work towards that goal in the future.*

Boss: *We like to promote people who are organized and tidy.*
Employee: *Yes, I will make those changes; thank you for drawing it to my attention.*
Boss: *I'm glad to hear it.*

Scripting

The broken record, fogging and negative assertion techniques are all appropriate for those situations in which you need to defend yourself from valid or invalid criticism. But what about those circumstances in which you need to initiate a discussion or express a critical view?

The **Scripting** technique is simple and effective. Here's how it works:

1. *You offer a brief summary of the situation.*
2. *Then you share your feelings about the situation. Take extra care to use the phrase 'I feel' and not 'You make me feel'.*
3. *Always acknowledge the other person's feelings.*
4. *State your goals and explain the desired outcome, but make sure these are realistic. If you have more than one or two requests, suggest that you arrange a time to meet for further discussion. If a compromise has not been reached, follow up with a letter detailing what's been discussed and including a statement that you still would like to negotiate further.*
5. *Outline how your ideas would benefit the other person. You may also include the negative consequences if he or she doesn't comply.*

Here are some examples of scripting in action:

'You criticized me in front of my colleagues this morning. I felt we could have discussed this issue in a more private place, and although I can appreciate there is cause for your annoyance, I would have preferred the discussion to take place in your office. There, we could have discussed the issues more calmly and I would have been able to concentrate more fully.'

'I asked you to have this report finished by this morning and it's still not complete. I felt I gave you sufficient time to work on it and I am now annoyed that it's not finished. I know that the report requires a lot of work, but if you had run into trouble with time or other commitments, then I would have liked you to tell me. That way, we both could have worked out a more realistic time frame.'

Some Further Help for Developing Assertiveness

1. Take a few moments to think about what you'd like to say. What is it that you're reacting to? What did the other person do or fail to do? Try not to jump to conclusions about the other person's intentions.

2. Don't assume that someone else can read your mind. The other person may not realize that he or she has upset or annoyed you. Clearing the air is the best way to resolve any issues and to prevent situations from getting worse.

3. Plan the most effective approach for expressing yourself. Be

*specific and address the problem at hand without introducing
any extraneous issues.*

4. *Don't blame or belittle the other person. He or she will only
become defensive and will be less likely to listen to you.*

5. *If you feel your message has not been heard, restate what
you'd like to say.*

Top Tips for Success

Taking the Tedium Out of Your Work Routine

Let's face it. Even the most exciting, glamorous and challenging
careers have their dull moments. If you find yourself stuck in a rut
or bogged down by paperwork, here's how to add some sparkle
and spice to the daily routine.

1. You're stuck working on a boring report for the next three
   months. However will you cope? Instead of focusing on the
   task in hand, think about the opportunity you've been given
   to develop an in-depth knowledge of the company you work
   for. Every career will have its less appealing downside, so
   you won't be alone. Just keep reminding yourself that this
   task adds to your knowledge base. Come promotion time,
   your new-found information will come in handy.

2. If you're stuck in the throes of some dull chore, rewarding
   yourself on a daily basis will keep you focused on the task.
   You deserve a special treat, so indulge.

3. Personalizing your work space, maybe even playing some background music, can help make the atmosphere more appealing and keep you motivated.

4. Think of ways to make boring work more stimulating, and make these suggestions to your boss. Task- or job-swapping will help reduce the monotony, for example, or working together in teams.

5. If you're stuck in the middle of a really – I mean brain-numbingly dull – task, then it's important to have something to look forward to. Meet up with friends for lunch or pamper yourself in the evening.

Taking the Sting Out of Criticism

It's not easy to inform a colleague that his or her work performance is substandard. Nor is it particularly pleasant when we're told that our work isn't up to scratch. However, on your road to success you will also have to learn the skills of doling out and receiving criticism.

In the best scenarios, criticism is meant to be constructive and will enable us to work more effectively. In the worst cases, critical appraisals will be destructive and meant as personal attacks. Unfortunately, there will be people who delight in putting you down. The working environment is called the rat race or a dog-eat-dog world sometimes for good reason. In either case, the way you manage giving and receiving criticism will speak volumes about your professional attitude.

Giving Criticism Effectively (and Painlessly!)

At times, we all come into contact with people whose actions or behaviours we find objectionable or unacceptable. It's important for all of us to offer criticism, to request changes, without hurting someone's feelings or leaving them feeling demeaned. We also wouldn't want to create a bad work atmosphere or cause arguments or needless fights.

However, telling a person something negative about their work performance or their behaviour is difficult for many. Sometimes it's easier to forego criticism, no matter how constructive and well-meaning, to avoid upsetting the other person or to prevent an unpleasant scene. So, we put up with an intolerable situation.

The reluctance to offer constructive criticism usually stems from many years of personally experiencing destructive criticism. If this sounds familiar, then the skills you will learn here aim to help you give constructive criticism. In other words, these tips will help you seek changes in someone else's behaviour without intentionally hurting the person's feelings or creating antagonism.

REASONS FOR GIVING CONSTRUCTIVE CRITICISM

1. *Some people may be unaware that their behaviour is offending those around them. As a result, their ability to interact and work successfully with others is impaired and this can lead to low staff morale and tension. By making people aware of their disagreeable behaviour – being*

chronically late, interrupting, borrowing things without permission – you will do them a favour in the long run.

2. If you fail to point out someone's unsatisfactory behaviour when required, you are likely to build up resentment and feel stressed and frustrated. As a result, your own behaviour could be negatively affected.

3. In being able to offer constructive criticism, you may not only produce positive changes in the other person's behaviour, you are also more likely to demonstrate to all your colleagues that you can handle a potentially difficult situation. Your staff or co-workers will appreciate your ability to communicate and feel more comfortable addressing problems with you in the future.

Lionel was a young attorney working for a busy corporate law firm. The pressures of his job meant that he needed to rely on the expertise of a competent legal secretary. Unfortunately, Suzanne wasn't really up to the job. Every week, it seemed she was coming into work complaining of a new personal catastrophe. Problems with her husband, her teenage daughter, the neighbours, finances and even her elderly parents meant that Suzanne was often distracted and unable to work efficiently.

Lionel's stress levels were increasing in proportion to Suzanne's latest crisis, but he felt unable to express his concerns that her personal problems were having an impact on his workload. Lionel didn't want to upset Suzanne, so he would listen patiently to her different crises and circle the mistakes she would make in her typing – hoping that Suzanne would get the hint that her work needed improvement. She *didn't. Then one day, Lionel was berated by a senior partner for the sloppiness in his correspondence to a client. Humiliated and angry, Lionel called Suzanne into his office and fired her on the spot – adding further to his secretary's problems.*

Was this the most effective way of handling this situation? No, of course not. Lionel chose a passive approach to the problem. In fact, he buried his head in the sand, just hoping the situation would improve on its own. In contrast, Suzanne assumed her boss was sympathetic to her woes and willingly helping her out by correcting her mistakes. Had Lionel set up a meeting with Suzanne, pointed out that her personal problems were interfering with her work performance and attempted to reach some kind of resolution, the situation would have progressed in a more positive direction.

Think about situations in your own life in which you needed to give constructive criticism. Did you react in a similar fashion to Lionel or were you more proactive? Were you able to avoid a deterioration of the situation or did matters become worse? Learning to give constructive criticism takes practice and experience.

GUIDELINES FOR GIVING CONSTRUCTIVE CRITICISM

1. *If you're angry or upset, take a few minutes and calm down before speaking. A shouting match will not help the situation.*
2. *Express your criticism in terms of your own personal feelings, and avoid facts or absolutes. Think about the*

following example. You and a colleague are meeting with prospective clients in the hope of generating new business. Although you both agree beforehand to contribute equally to the meeting, once it starts your colleague completely takes over. As a result, you sit there in silence, feeling totally unneccessary. If you confront your colleague by saying, 'How could you just ignore me like that? Your behaviour was inconsiderate and unprofessional,' then your criticism is stated in terms of facts and absolutes. As a result, your colleague is likely to respond in a defensive manner. Instead, by saying something along the lines of 'I felt disappointed that the meeting didn't progress as we had originally planned, and wonder if it's because I'm new to the company,' you are then able to express your feelings without antagonizing the other person.

3. *State your criticism in a clear, firm voice and avoid adopting an angry tone. If your criticism is expressed in the context of an angry outburst, it's less likely to be effective.*

4. *Criticize the behaviour, not the person. When people criticize us personally, insult us or call us names, we are much more likely to become defensive, un-cooperative and argumentative. Remember, just because someone engages in a behaviour or an action that we find questionable, this does not mean that the person is objectionable or bad.*

5. *Ask the person to change a specific behaviour. Sometimes we assume that people automatically know how to go about making changes in their behaviour. However, what may be completely obvious to us may be obscure to someone else, so you'll have to specify very carefully those changes you would like, and offer suggestions that will lead to improvement.*

Take the example of Lionel, the attorney. He resorted to circling Suzanne's spelling and grammatical errors on important documents. Instead, he could have asked her to use the spell check on her computer or have the office manager check over all correspondence and reports.

6. *Try to work out a compromise, if possible. The goal in offering constructive criticism is not to 'win', but to come up with a solution that is mutually satisfactory.*

7. *Always begin and end the conversation on a positive note. You will find that people are more likely to make alterations to their behaviour if they also hear positive comments about their work. Lionel might have made the following remarks to Suzanne: 'You've always been an efficient and thorough secretary, so I'm surprised that you've been making a lot of mistakes recently. I know you've been having many personal problems at home, but despite these difficulties you're a good employee and I know you'll be able to give the correspondence the detail it requires.'*

Receiving Criticism

If doling out criticism is difficult, receiving it is no picnic either. Critical comments, no matter how constructive, can seem hurtful and demeaning. However, since critical appraisals of our work are part and parcel of everyday life, learning to receive criticism with good grace is an impressive – and necessary – skill.

In learning to handle criticism of your work, you need to be able to see it not only as an opportunity to learn something valuable about yourself and how you affect other people – after all, most of us have room for improvement – you can also make positive changes that will help you achieve your goals.

Another reason to learn to receive criticism with dignity and a professional attitude is that doing so will help to reduce unnecessary arguments and tensions, and will demonstrate that you are receptive to other people's viewpoints. This will be essential for your career. If, instead, you respond in an angry manner to critical comments, other people will probably be less willing to approach you in future. On the surface this may seem desirable; most of us don't like people pointing out our shortcomings. However, defensive and angry reactions may hinder your professional growth and jeopardize career opportunities.

Remember, whether the criticism is constructive or destructive, always keep your cool. The comments might seem hurtful or demeaning, but you will do yourself no favours by responding in an emotional way or starting an argument.

I know first-hand how difficult it is to have a boss who is demeaning and destructive. A few years ago I worked in a child psychology department. My line manager was a few years younger than I was and kept reminding me how intimidated she was by my credentials, writing career and media activities. She was clearly a very insecure woman and she began abusing her position of authority. She belittled me privately and in front of colleagues, bombarded me with letters detailing how dissatisfied she was with my work and accused me of not following her instructions. Her comments were meant to be destructive and, at the time, they were very hurtful. I take pride in my professional work and was concerned that my reputation might be affected by this woman's malicious comments.

I responded by doing two things. First, I collected letters of reference from other people in the department I worked with, because I thought it was important to have documentation attesting to my professional conduct. And, second, I was always calm in my dealings with this woman. No matter how insulting or demeaning she became, I never reacted angrily or argued back. I stayed in that department for six months, and it wasn't easy. It was one of the most stressful periods of my working life. But, you know what? When I left once my contract was finished, my line manager's reputation suffered and I was complimented on my professional demeanour.

Dealing with Constructive and Destructive Criticism

1. *The main objective in being on the receiving end of destructive or constructive criticism is to prevent the situation from escalating into a fight. Be prepared to bite your tongue and hold back. Don't get defensive, don't argue back or counter-attack with criticisms of your own. Responding in an aggressive or hostile way won't be productive and will only guarantee that the lines of communication will shut down.*

2. *Do your best to find out and clarify all the information relating to the criticism. By asking for clarification and specifics, you are ensuring that the lines of communication stay open and can better ascertain why your work is considered unsatisfactory. As a result, your employer will be more likely to help you rectify the situation and offer you suggestions for improvement.*

3. *Try to identify some aspect of the criticism that you can agree with and are willing to change. After all, your employer might have a point and improvements might need to be made. Instead of responding in a hostile or defensive manner, own up and agree that certain aspects of your work could use more attention.*

4. *Suggest a solution that is mutually satisfactory. Usually, this will involve recognizing that some change in your behaviour is required.*

5. *Don't take any irrelevant, impertinent or unwarranted criticism personally. It's easy to take personal criticisms to heart. Learning to weed out the criticism that is meant to be helpful from that which is personally insulting will help keep things in perspective. Remember, just because someone comments on you as a person, it doesn't mean it's true.*

WHO HANDLES CRITICISM BETTER: MEN OR WOMEN?

In my work as a corporate consultant, I find that many people assume men can deal with criticism more effectively than women. It is sometimes assumed that men remain stoic and women burst into tears when receiving criticism. But are we just perpetuating sexist stereotypes? I think so.

I once had an interesting discussion with a psychology professor from Harvard University. Although this man hadn't conducted any systematic research on the subject at the time and his views were still at the hypothetical stage, he suggested that men were better equipped to handle criticism because they were more likely to participate in team sports as children. Since coaches are often critical in order to motivate their players, men become accustomed to negative comments about their performance from an early age.

I'm not sure I agree entirely with this man's views. After all, young women also participate in sports and their coaches are no less committed to excellence from their athletes. Based on my own experience in the corporate world, I have noticed very little difference in the way that men and women respond to criticism. When criticism is fair and constructive, both sexes tend to respond professionally and take positive action. However, when the comments are personal and destructive, most people, irrespective of their gender, feel upset and demeaned.

Top Tips for Success

Promotion Problems

CLIENT CONCERN

'I've just been offered a promotion at work, which I'm very excited about, particularly as it involves a lot of overseas travel. The only thing I'm worried about is that I've heard from colleagues that constant travelling can be tiring, stressful and lonely. I'm not so sure I want to accept the promotion now, but I'd hate to miss out on a great opportunity. What should I do?'

MY SOLUTION

Your promotion sounds exciting, so well done. Your company clearly regards your abilities highly, and your new responsibilities reflect their favourable impression.

Your ambivalent attitudes towards the travelling may reflect more than just your concerns about your new responsibilities. Your colleagues might be jealous that they've been passed over for promotion and are trying to convince themselves they didn't want the job anyway. Undermining your opportunity could be their way of making themselves feel better.

Your new job will require some adjustments, but how you adapt to the travelling will be more a product of your frame of mind. If you think it's an exciting opportunity to see some of the world and get to know other cultures, maybe learn a language, then you'll find this side of your new job an adventure. On the other hand, if you anticipate it will be boring and lonely, then you will probably find that that's the case.

Whether exciting or dull, you can learn a lot from these inter-national opportunities which will be selling points in times of pro-motion or if you find yourself looking for another job, so the opportunity itself has huge potential.

If you're still concerned, the best step to take is to finalize with your boss the amount of travel involved, including how often and for how long. Also, it's important to find out if you will be expected to travel during your own personal time. If all this is finalized in an acceptable way for you, why not give it a go?

24-Karat Conversations: Knowing What to Say and How to Say It

It's not always easy to pick up a telephone and speak to a total stranger, or walk into a room full of people you've never met and strike up a conversation. In fact, either scenario fills a lot of people with dread. They're too shy. They might make a fool of themselves. The conversation might dry up. They might stumble over their words or start babbling like an idiot.

Imaginary scenes of social disaster only needlessly fuel insecurities and hold people back. Learning good conversational skills, however, will be essential, and I mean absolutely essential, for achieving your ambitions. In order to get what you want out of life, you will have to express your goals, feel confident in approaching a wide range of people – many of whom will be powerful, intimidating and very busy – and develop social flair and confidence. Once you've truly mastered this art, people will be impressed by your ability and be more likely to help you. Believe you me, an articulate, socially savvy person generates excitement like nothing else.

Does the idea of approaching total strangers and initiating a conversation fill you with dread? If so, don't worry. Learning the fine art of conversation is easy. I promise.

Conversational Credibility

Talking to strangers and acquaintances – even impressive, influential ones – is not so nerve-wracking or difficult. A conversation is an important first step in establishing rapport and developing relationships with people. However, even if you doubt your conversational ability, don't despair. You are not alone. This is a difficult skill for many, but even shrinking violets can learn conversational ease.

Before we go any further, I want you to think about a variety of conversations you've had in the past. What conversations went well? Which were a disaster? Whom did you feel more comfortable speaking with? Whom did you dread having to talk with? How did you react when a conversation went badly? How did you feel when you decided to avoid a conversation with someone altogether? Most of us feel comfortable speaking with people we know well. We're relaxed and at ease. We also tend to enjoy those conversations that went well or have left us feeling positive in some way. In contrast, many people dread conversations with people they don't know well. Many shy away from approaching those in positions of power, or try to avoid conversations which are boring, demeaning or fill us with anxiety.

Developing Conversational Elegance

We've all had conversations which have made us feel interesting and even important. Likewise, most of us have found ourselves locked in discussions that have left us feeling devalued and uninteresting. Human nature being what it is, we often forget our conversational successes and focus on the failures.

So, before we continue I want you to think about a stressful conversation you've had with someone in which you felt the outcome was successful. Maybe it was a job interview or perhaps it was meeting your mother-in-law for the first time, or maybe a blind date. You decide. Now I want you to think about the emotions you felt right before the conversation started. Nervous? Intimidated? Anxious? Next, I want you to think about the development of the conversation and to identify the moment when you felt the outcome was going to be successful. How did you feel? Triumphant? Confident? Capable? My point here is that most of us have been forced to enter into conversations with intimidating people, yet, despite our nerves and reservations, we've managed to be successful.

Now think of a conversation that was a disaster. As I said earlier, I'm a firm believer in the phrase 'there's no failure, only feedback'. So, no matter how disastrous a meeting was, there's always something you can learn from the experience. Take my friend, Jean-Paul. We studied at Oxford together. Following the completion of his doctorate in history, Jean-Paul unfortunately had great difficulties securing a job. With a PhD from one of the world's most respected universities, he was at a loss to explain why he couldn't find work. One day I received a phone call from Jean-Paul in Canada. He was coming to England for a job interview at a university in London. Jean-Paul was excited and confident that he would be offered the position. He arrived in the UK and stayed with me. I asked him if he needed time to prepare for the interview and he said no, as he was convinced the position was in the bag. A native French speaker, I also noticed that his English wasn't quite fluent, but he insisted upon spending time with French-speaking friends visiting from Paris.

When the big day came, I received a call from Jean-Paul immediately following the interview. It had been a disaster and Jean-Paul felt humiliated and distraught. His lack of preparation meant he was unfamiliar with the latest trends in his field. His faulty English meant he had problems expressing himself and he stumbled over his words. When Jean-Paul returned to my house, I knew he needed some sympathy and kid-glove treatment, but we also talked about what he'd learned from this interview experience. He vowed never again to be so arrogant and ill-prepared. A few weeks later, Jean-Paul called to tell me he had been offered another job.

Ice-breakers and Conversation Starters

Jean-Paul was able to learn something valuable from his difficult interview experience, but his is not the only type of awkward social exchange. Without doubt, the majority of people I encounter complain that they don't know what to say when striking up a conversation with someone for the first time. They're also afraid they'll run out of topics of conversation and start babbling, leaving a very bad impression.

So, what should people talk about? When we meet people, particularly those we want to impress, we want to come across well and avoid topics that might cause offence. When people are nervous, they notoriously put their foot in their mouth and can insult a new acquaintance without even being aware of it. However, some topics, traditionally thought of as taboo, are perfectly acceptable. Let's take a look at some of the more common misunderstandings about starting a conversation.

You Should Only Discuss 'Important' Topics of Conversation

Actually, it isn't necessary to begin a conversation by discussing the threat to the environment, worldwide hunger or the exploitation of the developing world. It's not your role, here, to try to solve all the world's problems. In fact, particularly if you or someone else has strong views on a subject, you might run the risk of antagonizing the situation.

Conversations, especially with people you don't know very well, should be light-hearted, fun and an exchange of information. In other words, small talk is acceptable and desirable. You might want to begin with a topic the other person has some familiarity with, so that they can respond easily. People you know in common, a recent sporting event, even the weather are all good conversation starters.

You, Alone, Are Responsible for Maintaining the Conversation

When I ask people what is their biggest fear about striking up a conversation with someone they've only recently met, invariably they're anxious that the conversation will fizzle out. Remember, a conversation is a two-way process and, at most, you're only responsible for 50 per cent of the effort. If the discussion starts to flag despite your best efforts, then make your excuses and leave.

You Must Never Talk About Yourself

Many of us are raised to believe that talking about ourselves is rude and immodest. As a result, we often feel more comfortable asking other people about themselves, their likes and their interests. However, the best way to find out if you share common interests and likes and dislikes is to tell others about yours. Besides, psychological research has demonstrated that if you disclose information about yourself, other people will feel more comfortable about doing the same. Just be careful not to hog the conversation.

MORE HELP FOR CONFIDENT CONVERSATIONS

1. *Listen to others and observe them. We can pick up all kinds of cues from other people about good topics of conversation. Do they respond enthusiastically to something we say, or do they appear bored?*

2. Never attempt to begin a conversation with someone who is busy, in a hurry, or already engaged in a discussion with others. If you're eager to join a group, wait until there is a lull in the conversation before you speak. You don't have to be hesitant, just don't barge in.

3. Use open-ended questions, because they will encourage a response. In contrast, closed questions will only get you a 'yes' or 'no' answer, leading to a dead-end conversation. 'What did you like about the novel?' versus 'Did you like the novel?', for example, will signal to the other person you're interested in his or her views and want to speak further.

4. Make sure the other person is interested in your conversation. Sometimes conversations run their course very quickly, or maybe the other person is keen to speak with someone else and feels awkward about interrupting your flow. It will do you no favours to ramble on to a bored audience. How is the other person responding? Are their answers to your questions becoming shorter? Are they looking at their watch, glancing around the room, fiddling with their jewellery? Remember, conversations should be enjoyable and easy. If you find the other person has become distracted, it's time to end the conversation.

5. Finish the conversation gracefully. When the conversation first shows the signs of waning, it's time to end the exchange. You can extricate yourself by simply saying you've got to be going, or you've promised to speak with the host about a particular matter or that you've just spotted a friend you haven't seen in a while. The important thing is to give the impression that you've enjoyed speaking with the other person.

Top Tips for Success

Silver Service Guaranteed

Whether you're out for a night on the town with your friends or keen to impress a new client, you can appreciate the importance of good service. When busy bartenders, waiters or maitre d's treat us like VIPs, we and our guests feel special. If, however, there is a bad rapport with staff, the potential disasters are too numerous to mention. Suffice it to say, you are likely to feel ignored or embarrassed. What will that do to your reputation?

1. Competition for taxis can be fierce. So, hail a taxi when five other people are also clambering around, and you'll really stand out as a winner. Taxi drivers say they're more willing to pick up someone who smiles and appears friendly. Also, make eye contact with the driver and wave. Otherwise, he'll think you're calling out to a friend.

2. I've been in so many situations where my host, eager to impress, treats the restaurant staff like dirt. Never, ever, ever patronize or insult a waiter or bartender. You'll never know what filth ends up in your dinner or drink. And you just might end up wearing what you've ordered. Instead, being friendly on arrival will ensure you good service.

3. Learning the bartender's name, leaving a tip or buying him a drink will help guarantee you'll get his attention when there's a crowd at the bar.

4. Always, always acknowledge good service. Even a simple please and thank you will work wonders.

Complimentary Therapy: Giving and Receiving Praise Gracefully

On your climb up the ladder of success, two things will invariably happen. First, you will need to appreciate the efforts and assistance of others who have helped you along the way. And second, you will have to become accustomed to the praise of others when they recognize your hard work and commitment.

Giving Compliments

The satisfaction we derive from our personal and professional relationships depends, at least in part, on feeling comfortable sharing positive things with them. Whether it's the secretary who's worked extra hard to type up a last-minute report, the family friend who's introduced us to a useful contact, the co-worker who covered for us when we were late back to the office from lunch, the partner who is supportive of our long work hours or our parents who look after our children when we have a late business meeting, there are lots of people who deserve our gratitude and thanks.

Giving compliments and showing appreciation are necessary requirements for building and maintaining our relationships. But we often fail to express our thanks. Sometimes, we assume it's understood. Other times, we start to take our friends and family for granted. Or maybe we're uncomfortable about sharing our feelings with others. Perhaps we feel more comfortable receiving compliments. Whatever your reservations, it is possible to express your appreciation without embarrassing yourself or others.

Paying Compliments Successfully

1. *Try to phrase your compliment in terms of your own feelings. When you say, 'I really appreciated your introducing me to your cousin, the managing director of the company I want to work for,' this conveys warmth and gratitude. In contrast, saying 'The meeting with the managing director was a huge success' fails to acknowledge the other person's efforts. While both sentences are positive, the first is more personal and heartfelt.*

2. *Be specific when you give a compliment. When you are specific in your praise for someone, it demonstrates that you've taken the time to notice exactly how they've helped you out. Although receiving a general compliment like 'I really enjoy working with you' will be received well, it's also important to recognize when someone has made an extra effort to assist and support you.*

3. *A sentence or two will be adequate. Remember, this is not a 'This is your Life' moment, nor is it an Academy Award ceremony. There is no need to gush. A simple: 'Thanks for helping me out with that project the other night. I know you had to cancel your plans and I appreciate the trouble you went to' is all that will be required.*

4. *When in doubt, say it with flowers. OK, so you're no Peter Ustinov and speeches aren't your thing. There are other ways to show your appreciation. Flowers, chocolates or a bottle of wine also achieve the same goal.*

5. *Be sincere. There's nothing more insulting than an insincere, saccharine 'compliment'. So, only offer a compliment if you truly mean it. Otherwise, people will see through it and think you're up to something.*

Think about a situation in which you complimented someone you know. Perhaps they helped you out, or maybe you just liked the necklace they were wearing. The exact situation isn't so important. When you've identified a situation, ask yourself how you felt at the time. Was giving a compliment easy or difficult? Did you overpraise the person or did you mumble under your breath? How did the other person react to your comments?

Receiving Compliments

Receiving compliments with grace and without embarrassment is also essential when you're achieving your ambitions. If you handle praise a little too well, you may come across as arrogant, ungracious and conceited. In contrast, if you feel awkward when someone compliments you on a job well done, you might convey the impression that you're insecure, awkward and self-conscious.

In either event, you won't do your career much good, I'm afraid. But, striking the right balance is achievable, with just a little practice.

One of my clients, called Carol, had recently begun a new job in an investment bank, working in quantitative analysis. Eager to fit in with her colleagues and impress her boss, Carol volunteered to stay late, to help her co-workers when they got stuck running computer programmes, and to edit a report for head office. Both numerate and literate, Carol possessed a number of a impressive skills, and it wasn't long before her efforts were noticed. However, instead of gaining the respect of those she worked with, Carol was soon in danger of becoming the office joke. You see, every time Carol was praised for a job well done, she belittled her efforts. Not wishing to come across as arrogant, Carol responded to compliments with 'I didn't really help all that much' or 'Anyone else could have done the same thing.' When Carol de-valued her own efforts, irrespective of her motives, her co-workers began to do the same. Instead of gaining a reputation as a dedicated high flier, people began to question whether Carol was worthy of her status and big salary.

Complimentary Therapy

Graciously Accept

1. *Don't negate the compliment or dismiss the praise. When someone gives you a compliment, accept it and thank the person. For example, if someone compliments you on an outfit you're wearing and you respond by saying, 'This old suit? It was really cheap, I got it on sale. In fact, I was toying with the idea of giving it to charity,' you not only put yourself down, but also insult the other person. Basically, you will have implied that neither you nor the other person has any sense of style and that the other's opinions aren't valid. A simple 'thank you' will convey graciousness on your part and validate the other person's views. Both of you will feel like winners.*

2. *Indicate that you appreciate the compliment, even if you don't agree with it. You may feel that accepting a compliment you don't deserve is somehow dishonest. It's not. It's the sentiment behind the comment you will be responding to. By saying 'Thank you, that's nice of you to say,' you convey to the other person that you appreciate their remarks, without implying that you share their views.*

Top Tips for Success

Simple Solutions to Everyday Problems

1. If a difficult situation arises at work, don't instantly panic. You might just be overreacting. So, be honest with yourself.

Is it a **real** problem worth fretting over? Your secretary who occasionally comes back to the office late is not a problem. Someone who repeatedly misses deadlines is.

2. Don't bottle up your concerns. You'll only feel stressed. Instead, talk about the problem with a friend, acquaintance or even a stranger. Don't ignore your gut feelings, though – our instincts are generally right.

3. Don't lose it over minor matters. If your secretary's desk is a mess and it makes it difficult for you to find files, etc., there's no need to explode. She (or he!) may not have even realized that you were annoyed.

(Listen to Madonna and)
Express Yourself

We all have feelings. In common with our fellow man and woman, we've all experienced anger, frustration, guilt, happiness, enthusiasm, relief and fear at some point or another. Emotional reactions usually vary from person to person. Some people react more intensely and more frequently to emotional situations than others. Some tend to bottle up their feelings and deal with them privately.

In networking and building contacts, it will be essential to share your feelings, your opinions and your ideas openly with other people. If you tend to keep your feelings to yourself, then the idea of opening up and expressing your opinions probably fills you with dread. Don't worry. Many people are in the same boat. Sharing what you think and how you feel is an important communication skill that can be developed. It just takes a little bit of know-how and some practice. Then, after a while, it will seem like second nature.

The Benefits of Expressing Yourself

1. *People who come across as shy or those who keep their opinions firmly to themselves are often perceived as cold, aloof and arrogant. As a result, others may avoid them or feel awkward engaging them in conversations. You cannot afford to discourage people from approaching you.*

2. *Sharing your opinions and your feelings will help you develop deeper relationships with others. When we're candid in our views and move beyond the small-talk stage, our relationships also move on.*

3. *When you open up and reveal your true thoughts and feelings, you let others know that it's OK for them to do the same. Being candid like this is a great way of building trust, rapport and even affection.*

4. *Sharing your personal views and opinions is also a great way of offering support to someone else. If you're angry or upset about a situation, chances are other people are as well. Why suffer in silence alone, when you can be united in support?*

How do you feel about speaking your mind? Do you think of times when you were dying to say something, but couldn't? Or can you think of a moment when you were a bit too frank and someone became offended by your comments? Learning to strike the right balance isn't easy.

Madolyn learned this lesson the hard way. She had been working as a teacher for seven years and decided she no longer wanted to help shape the minds of the future. For a year or so, Madolyn had been thinking about working in public relations,

*but had absolutely no idea how to break into the field.
Madolyn's mother, however, knew of someone who knew of
someone else who worked in PR, and this man agreed to set up
a meeting with Madolyn.*

*Madolyn realized that her mother's acquaintance could
turn out to be an important contact, so she was keen to appear
appreciative and pleasant. Unfortunately, this man was
currently undergoing a divorce and was more keen to discuss
his break-up than careers in public relations. In fact, Madolyn
appeared so sympathetic that this man set up a series of
meetings, ostensibly to discuss PR. However, his real intention
was to talk about the divorce and custody battle he was facing.
Madolyn was genuinely receptive to listening to his problems —
after all, he was also supposed to help her. So, at first, she
thought this was an even exchange. But every time she tried to
draw the conversation around to her career, nothing doing.
After four meetings and no discussions about jobs in PR,
Madolyn was beginning to feel used.*

*Still hopeful to keep him as a contact, however, Madolyn
continued to offer advice and support. Then, one day, this man
became very upset. He had just found out that the divorce was
going through and his wife was gaining custody of the
children. What's worse, he criticized Madolyn, accusing her of
giving bad advice. Stunned, but fed up, Madolyn made her
excuses and left — none the wiser about landing a career in
public relations.*

Madolyn, like many people, was raised to be considerate and
polite. She was taught, from an early age, that expressing her
opinions or feelings was impertinent. While it's important never

to be aggressive or rude, Madolyn learned the hard way that she was being exploited. She came to me in tears, feeling angry, frustrated and used. But she had learned a valuable lesson. She learned to establish boundaries with others and became more confident as a result.

How to Express Your Feelings

1. *It's acceptable to reveal how you feel. As long as you remain calm and avoid offending the other person, expressing your thoughts and feelings will establish boundaries and gain you respect. If others know what your limits are, they won't be able to push you around or take advantage.*

2. *Share both positive and negative feelings. Most of us have been taught that if you can't say something nice, then you shouldn't say anything at all. But no one is happy all the time, and negative emotions just fester unless they are expressed. By learning to talk openly about a wide range of emotions, people will know where they stand with you and your relationships will flourish.*

3. *Understand the limitations. Your goal here is not to reveal all your deepest, most personal thoughts and feelings with absolutely everyone that comes down the pike. Nor is it to go running off at the mouth with the first person who comes along. There are different levels of emotions and you will confide in some people more than others. Gauge your reactions accordingly.*

Top Tips for Success

Multi-cultural Cordiality

With the rise of the global economy there are more and more opportunities to work with overseas clients. While international travel and visiting new cultures can be exciting, you have to take extra care not to offend. What's acceptable behaviour in one culture can be quite obscene in another.

Winston Churchill learned this important lesson. Upon arriving in Greece following the end of the Second World War, Churchill was met by a throng of locals. Much to his shock, the crowd greeted him with what to him, as a Briton, was an obscene hand gesture – two fingers in the air, the backs of their hands facing him. However, the Greeks were actually being respectful. In their culture, exposing the palm of your hand to someone is considered rude. Because they wanted to give Churchill a warm welcome and avoid offence, they concealed their palms when greeting him with his own 'V for victory' sign. As a result, the gesture, which was meant to be respectful, was instead inadvertently profane.

It's so easy to insult someone unknowingly from a different culture. Because our diplomats have enough on their plates, you don't want to cause any international incidents when you go abroad. If in doubt, always contact the consulate of the country you're planning to visit and ask for guidance on acceptable behaviour.

Are You Listening?

Now that you've outlined your goals and ambitions, you're probably very excited at the thought of going out and pursuing them. You also probably (and understandably!) hope that others share your enthusiasm. However, in your quest for success you'll need to take the advice of all kinds of people – even if it means they don't always tell you what you want to hear. You might think you're the millennium's answer to Gwyneth Paltrow, but maybe your acting skills aren't up to scratch. You may be convinced your new fashion design venture is a guaranteed roaring success, but you'll also need to brush up on the less glamorous side of business – like bookkeeping and ordering paper for the photocopier.

My point is, no matter what your goals you will benefit enormously from the advice of people who know the score. Whether they're family members and friends who are trying to steer you in the right direction or an expert with years of experience in your field, developing good listening skills will pay dividends.

Not only will you be able to pursue your goals faster, you'll also learn to recognize the people who have your best interests at heart.

I don't mean to be negative, but, let's face it: Not everyone will be thrilled with your new-found goals. Your success might just very well remind someone else that their life is monotonous and dull. You won't be welcomed with open arms by others who already feel the bite of competition at their heels. Even when advice is well-meaning, the recommendations offered could be worthless – setting you back. In making the right choices, you'll need to be discerning.

Distinguishing good advice from bad begins with listening. And I don't just mean letting the other person speak while you're waiting to have a go. No. Listening attentively is a proactive skill, not a passive one. It involves actively paying attention to what the other person is saying (and in some cases, not saying) and understanding what he or she is trying to communicate.

Sometimes our advisors will be direct. At other times their message will be very subtle.

Jonathan learned the importance of attentive listening, but it took him three years of unemployment to do so. Jonathan had been working in academia, as a mathematician, but found his career potential was limited. Jobs were few and he didn't relish spending the rest of his life teaching a bunch of bored undergraduates. Jonathan knew that investment banks were crying out for his skills, so he assumed that securing a position would be a breeze. Several interviews later, however, Jonathan was still at the ivory tower. He just couldn't figure it out. Then, at one interview, the personnel manager finally clued him in.

She said she didn't know if Jonathan would be invited back for another interview, but in future she would advise him to be more forthcoming with his responses and to look the interviewer in the eye when speaking.

Jonathan was affronted by this woman's disclosure. After all, who was she to question him – a doctor of mathematics at Oxford. When he phoned me up he was in a foul temper, but I suggested we analyse this woman's comments dispassionately. Upon doing so, Jonathan revealed that he behaved the same way in all interviews. Assuming that his qualifications were the sole focus of discussion, Jonathan made little effort to engage with the interviewers. He didn't mean to appear arrogant; he was just naive. Not the most socially adept person to begin with, Jonathan's work – either at the university or at a bank – would be solitary anyway. People skills were not a requirement per se. However, Jonathan learned the hard way that even his high-level degrees weren't sufficient. What's more, upon even closer inspection Jonathan realized that several previous interviewers had been trying to drop hints about his seemingly unfriendly behaviour. He just hadn't picked them up.

Following our conversation, Jonathan decided to pay attention to this interviewer's advice. He wasn't called back for another interview, but he landed the very next job. He still works on his own, but he's learned the value of improving his communication skills.

Reading Others

Improving Body Talk

PAY ATTENTION TO POSTURE

People often either slouch or come across as stiff and rigid. It's important that you adopt a relaxed posture. When you convey the message that you are relaxed, other people will find it easier to approach you.

Try these tips. When you're sitting down, rest your back against the chair and keep your arms either folded across your body or place them on the arm rests. You'll feel – and look – more relaxed.

When you're standing up, you can also easily adopt a relaxed posture just by distributing your weight evenly. In doing so you stop yourself from swaying or rocking back and forth, which is not only distracting but can give the message that you're nervous and uncomfortable. Take care that you're not standing too rigidly, however. The message you are likely to convey if you stand too rigidly is that you are intimidating and inflexible.

Another undesirable message that poor posture can convey is shyness or insecurity. To convey social confidence you should sit or stand directly in front of the person/people, or perhaps at just a slight angle. Remember to relax. If you're too stiff, you could come across as confrontational!

PERSONAL SPACE

When you're speaking to someone it's also important to monitor your personal space. If you stand too close, others will feel crowded and invaded. As a result, your listeners will become anxious and will do their best to move away from you. Will they hear anything you've said? Not a chance.

If you stand too far away, you will convey distance and lack of interest. In the worst case scenario you'll come across as a Howard Hughes, in fear of contamination. In either case, not the best way to win support.

Although it varies from culture to culture, the best rule of thumb for personal space is to keep a distance of about 60 centimetres/2 feet.

EYE CONTACT

Remember my acquaintance Jonathan from the last chapter? He learned a valuable lesson about eye contact. Eye contact is of course a two-way process; it's just as important to initiate it as it is to receive it when you're talking to others. When you maintain eye contact, you convey to the other person that you're interested in the conversation and are following what's being said.

While eye contact is a great way of ensuring mutual attention in a conversation, be careful not to overdo it. You may come across as staring or aggressive, and the other person will feel anxious and uncomfortable.

To strike the right balance during a conversation, you should maintain eye contact about half the time.

Reading Others

TONE OF VOICE

The tonal quality of your voice will also need care. What kind of message will you convey if you sound hostile and sarcastic? What about cold and superior? Or weak and hesitant? The same words take on completely different meanings. Your tone of voice should sound relaxed, confident and warm.

FACIAL EXPRESSION

Our faces convey a significant proportion of our reactions, so it's important that our facial expressions are congruous with our words. Also, if you maintain an open, warm and friendly expression on your face, it conveys to the other person that you are enjoying the conversation. If, however, you tend to frown or scowl, these negative expressions will be interpreted as discouraging or disapproving. Are they likely to enhance the conversation? Probably not.

NODDING YOUR HEAD

An easy way to demonstrate your interest when conversing with someone is to nod your head. You will show the other person that you're following the conversation and that you're encouraging him or her to continue. Just be careful you don't overdo it. Excessive head bobbing can be pretty distracting and off-putting!

NERVOUS HABITS

We all have them. Whether it's fiddling with your hair, playing with your ring, licking your lips, clicking a pen on and off or shifting awkwardly in a chair, you indicate to others that you're uncomfortable and would rather be elsewhere. Becoming aware of these nervous gestures is the first step to controlling them. If you're a pen clicker, then put the ballpoint out of reach. If you play with your hair, make sure it's tied back and out of the way. If you're a ring-turner, concentrate on resting your hands in your lap. You want your audience to be focusing on you, not on your anxieties!

The first step in improving your nonverbal skills is to take a good, hard look at the way you communicate with others. Do you avoid eye contact with people you don't know very well? Do you slouch like a shrinking violet? Do you mumble so others have to ask you three times to repeat yourself? Do you bounce in and crowd someone's personal space? Do you bray like a donkey every time you hear a funny joke? If you're not sure, ask a friend to be honest and constructive. Remember, this is for your benefit. In pursuing your goals you won't just need to *sound* articulate and confident, you'll have to convey it. And, without a doubt, when it comes to communicating effectively with others, our body language often speaks louder than words.

Best Foot Forward

Studies have shown us time and time again that people make quick judgments about one another. And, I mean **very** quick. Thirty seconds to a minute is all it takes for someone else to size us up and decide whether or not we've made the grade. You won't be given a second chance to make a good impression, so the first one's got to be spot on.

It may be wrong to judge a book by its cover. But in this busy, competitive world, looking the part is usually equated with being the part. Successful people understand the importance of managing the impression they give to others. Would you trust your doctor if she or he turned up looking scruffy and messy? Would you accept your accountant's guarantee of his or her painstaking attention to detail if the office looked like a monsoon had struck? Would you trust your crowning glory to a hairdresser whose own appearance was slovenly and unkempt? Probably not. Of course, all of these people might be at the top of their field, even if their image is dubious. One of my dons at Oxford was routinely mistaken for a tramp, but this didn't stop him from being a highly acclaimed expert in his field.

Oxford academics aside, my point is this: Image may not be everything, but it counts for a lot. Studies have repeatedly shown that potential employers make up their minds about hiring a candidate within seconds of meeting them. Likewise, when people are being considered for promotion, research has also found that their performance counts only for about 10 per cent, while image and visibility within the company amount to 90 per cent.

How Men and Women Are Perceived Differently at Work

Family Photos on the Desk

Men: He's working hard to support his family.
Women: She'd rather be at home with her children.

A Cluttered Desk

Men: He's in charge of lots of projects.
Women: She's messy and disorganized.

Being Away from Their Desk

Men: He's in a business meeting.
Women: She's in the Ladies' Room.

Talking to Colleagues

Men: He's obviously discussing an important project detail with colleagues.
Women: She's gossiping.

Lunching with the Boss

Men: He and the boss are discussing career potential and promotion opportunities.
Women: She and the boss are having an affair.

Is it a shallow world? Yes, and it's also unfair and rife with prejudices. I don't mean to sound jaded, but you can't assume that your hard work or innate talents alone will guarantee you the success you crave. When it comes to your image, forewarned is forearmed.

Why don't we take a look at the impact your image makes on your life? Right now, think of three different occasions when you felt you made a good impression. Maybe it was a job interview, a first date or a meeting with your prospective in-laws. Reflecting on each occasion, ask yourself the following questions:

1. *What image were you trying to convey?*
2. *How did you feel before you arrived?*
3. *What was the outcome you were hoping for?*
4. *In what ways did you change your behaviour to suit the occasion?*
5. *Did you make a special effort with your appearance?*
6. *What do you think accounts for the outcome that was achieved?*

Once you've completed this exercise, I want you to think about three different scenarios when you felt you made a bad impression. Go through the same series of questions, but also ask yourself if you could have rectified the situation in any way. Maybe you were half an hour late for an interview, perhaps that joke that seemed so funny when your friend told it the other night fell completely flat, or maybe you inadvertently put your foot in your mouth with an unsuitable comment. I'd bet that unless you were extremely lucky or the other person was particularly sympathetic, there was no turning back from the bad impression.

Top Tips for Success

Re-entering the Workforce after a Break

Maybe you decided to travel around the world for a year or two, pursue a degree or take time off to have a baby. You're now keen to re-enter the workforce and resume your career, but returning –

even after a relatively short break – can be a daunting experience. Cosy little offices have been replaced by impersonal open-plan work stations. Dress-down Fridays have revolutionized office attire. Permanent jobs have made way for temporary contracts. To cut down on the culture shock and update your skills, think about the following tips.

1. Pay a visit to a recruitment agency. They'll have a look at your CV and quickly fill you in on the job opportunities for people with your skills and qualifications.

2. If you've been away from the office for some time, you'll probably have to take a refresher course and update your computer skills.

3. Re-entering the job force is the perfect time to decide if you want to continue with your former career or think about new opportunities. You may want to discuss any new interests with a human resources manager.

4. Don't be put off applying for a job because of family and child commitments. There's much more flexibility nowadays and job-sharing is on the rise.

5. You'll need to find out what's been going on in your field since you've been away. Trade journals are a vital source of information.

6. If you're not sure you want to make a full-time commitment, talk to your boss about working maybe one day a week or coming on board in a consultant's capacity.

7. Returning to work, if you've got child commitments, will mean huge changes to the family. Women often feel that it's their sole responsibility to take care of the home when they go back to work. No way. That superwoman ideal we

strive for is a myth. You can't do it on your own. Your partner and children will also have to muck in.

8. Don't undervalue the skills you've acquired since you've been away from the workplace. Parenting, travelling and/or pursuing further education require many skills that are valuable in the workplace. Don't discount them.

9. If you return to work at the same company as before, accept that changes will have been made and be willing to learn new office routines and procedures.

10. Consider the temping option. Temping is a great way to try out different companies until you find one that suits you, your skills and your other commitments.

Dress for Success

Since looking the part is essential, you will need to pay particular attention to your appearance. While fine feathers don't always make fine birds, the clothes you choose to wear convey more than just your personal style. They convey credibility.

The 'dress for success' slogan may seem like a relic from the 1980s, but the message is just as relevant to us now.

When deciding on your professional wardrobe, the first question you will need to ask yourself is: What impression am I trying to project? Authority? Creativity? Concern? Ability? Energy? Confidence? Team player?

If you've identified the image you desire but don't know how to go about achieving the look, don't worry. It's easy. The first thing to do is to think of someone who shares the same kind of image that you'd like to project. Maybe it's a senior manager at work or the kooky, creative friend of your sister's. Next, analyse what it is about their wardrobe and personal style that conveys a certain image. With the senior manager, it could be her understated elegance, choice of conservative colours, finely tailored suits, minimal jewellery or expensive designer shoes. With someone more creative you might be drawn to their daring colour combinations, the trendiness of their outfits, their youthful, energetic style or in-your-face attitude. Remember, the point is to select clothes that represent your image, not just your personal style. Save that for your weekend wardrobe.

But what if you've just found out you have a job interview and have no idea what the dress codes are? Not to worry. The smart money is on hanging out in front of the office building – during lunch hour or closing time – and having a good look at what the other employees are wearing.

If someone in a similar position carries a briefcase, dresses conservatively and wears a skirt, come interview time you'd better look the same. I'm not suggesting you have to be a carbon copy, but companies look for employees who are going to fit in and not cause trouble. As I said before, if you want the job, you'll have to look the part.

The Art of Successful Dressing

Even if your style has been described as 'anti-style', it's really easy to dress well. With a little attention to detail you can develop a professional image in no time. It doesn't matter if your chosen profession is creative or conservative. Wherever you'd like to work, you'll be a fashion success if you ensure that your clothes:

- *help you feel confident*
- *fit well and flatter your figure*
- *reflect your position within the company and the responsibilities you have*
- *complement your hair, eye and skin colour*
- *help you project the image you wish to convey.*

Don't forget your hair and make-up! There won't be much point in investing in a good wardrobe if you neglect these other areas of your appearance.

If you haven't stepped foot into a salon or bought new make-up in years, don't worry. Make an appointment with a *respectable* – and, be warned, this will mean expensive – hair salon for a consultation and visit the cosmetics counter of a *good* department store for some basics. You'll be on the right track before long. Just be sure you make clear the image you want to project!

Improving Your Professional Communication Skills

In the professional world you have to interact with people all the time. Letters, e-mails, telephone calls, faxes, interviews, meetings and one-to-one contact all involve interacting with co-workers and other professionals. Here are some of the many reasons why effective, professional communication skills strengthen organizations:

- *People feel motivated.*
- *Misunderstandings decrease.*
- *Colleagues listen.*
- *Team work is more effective.*
- *Time and money can be saved.*
- *Deadlines are met.*
- *Important information and resources can be shared.*
- *You and others feel empowered.*

- *You reinforce to others your leadership abilities and your professionalism.*
- *You develop credibility and inspire confidence in others.*

When we're involved in a communication process that promotes understanding, we all work more efficiently and are more confident that we're on the right track. Can you think of an example in which the channels of communication were clear and successful? What were the benefits to you and your organization?

No doubt, you can identify many such examples. Unfortunately, the business world is not perfect and the communication process in the workplace can lead to ambiguities and even break down altogether. Can you think of a situation in which the channels of communication failed to work? Maybe it was a memo from your boss. Perhaps a letter or a telephone call that was unclear. Maybe one of your colleagues was supposed to book a room for a meeting and didn't. What was the effect of this breakdown on you and the others you worked with?

In some cases the consequences are minor and easily rectified. In others, however, your professional reputation may have been put on the line. Here are some of the more common disasters that occur when communication is ineffective:

- *People look inept and unprofessional.*
- *Confidence in someone's ability is lost.*
- *Money and time are wasted.*
- *Stress and frustration levels are raised.*
- *Delays are likely to result.*
- *Morale is impaired.*
- *Someone may lose their job.*

Keep It Simple, Sister

Most of us have been in situations where communication has been effective. We've also seen the disasters that result when the process has broken down. So, what's the best way of making sure the process runs smoothly?

Easy. It's the **KISS** principle. In other words, **K**eep **I**t **S**imple, **S**ister.

When communicating in the professional world, there are only three points you need to remember:

1. *Clearly define the purpose or message you wish to send.*
2. *Take account of the audience/reader/listener and their time, level of involvement and knowledge about the situation.*
3. *Make sure the sentences are short and the wording easy to understand.*

Your colleagues and clients will be bombarded with countless memos, e-mails, phone calls and faxes throughout the busy work day. There is only so much stimulus the brain can handle, and your various communications will be in competition with everyone else's. By following the KISS principle and adhering to the three rules outlined above, you will increase the effectiveness of your communications and reduce the possibility of mistakes.

When in Doubt, Think of the Five Ws

Making sure the structure of your correspondence is simple and easy to follow is just as important as the wording. Stick to the five **W**s – **W**ho, **W**hat, **W**hy, **W**hen and **W**here – and your message will practically write itself.

Dear Bob,

I would like to arrange a meeting with you to discuss the progress of the report we've been working on. I am free on Tuesday afternoon. I hope my office will be convenient. Please call to confirm.

OTHER CONSIDERATIONS

- *Is your message confidential?*
- *Do you want a record of your message?*
- *Is the message formal or informal?*
- *Do you expect a response?*
- *Will your message be aimed at one person or several?*
- *Is there the chance that the information you've sent might be used inappropriately?*
- *Is the message urgent?*

Setting the Right Tone

When speaking or writing to people, you'll want to ensure that the communication is positively received and that you've projected a favourable image. Extra care must be taken in case you accidentally annoy or offend someone you work with. Here are some of the top turn-offs:

- *adopting too informal a tone*
- *appearing demeaning or patronizing*
- *making unfair demands*
- *sending offensive or inappropriate material*
- *bombarding people with unnecessary calls, memos or e-mails*
- *grammatical errors and misspelled words.*

If any of these communication turn-offs ring true with you, then it's time for a rethink. Carry on this way and you'll be committing professional suicide. The tone of a message, whether written or oral, can convey warmth, gratitude, authority, encouragement and praise. Successful people understand full well that every message they send out reflects their image. And that even the briefest of memos will enhance or hurt their professional reputation.

Words to the Wise

When you're writing a memo, fax, e-mail or letter, be prepared to take some time, organize your thoughts and carefully select the language you want to use.

I recommend starting with an outline and working on a few drafts. By carefully thinking about your message and polishing the style, you will come across as professional, confident and capable. The more you practise, the easier it will become. And remember, the recipient won't know that you've invested your time. They'll think you've whipped the message up and be impressed at your succinctness and flair!

Don't Forget the Details

Imagine the scenario: Your message is simply stated and the tone is warm, deferential and clear. Your wording is consistent, your objectives are well defined. What could go wrong? Plenty. Many people get to this point and they become sloppy. Believe you me, it's the fine details that will make all the difference.

Always, Always, Always

- *Make sure you've spelled the person's name correctly.*
- *Check and double-check their title and address.*
- *Put the document through a spell and grammar check.*
- *Make sure your data is factual and correct.*
- *Look out for spill marks or smudges.*
- *Make sure the printer, photocopier or typewriter (some people still use them!) produces a professional, clean document.*

Top Tips for Success

What to Do When the Boss Undermines You

CLIENT CONCERN

'I work in a human resources department for a big multi-national company. As a rule, my boss is very easy-going and we get on well most of the time, except when we're in meetings.

When I give my opinion in a meeting, particularly when senior managers are present, she undermines me. She dismisses everything I say, speaks over me, shakes her head in disagreement even before I get the words out of my mouth. She even criticizes me for the mistakes she's made. The funny thing is, once the meeting's over she's her old easy-going self again. I don't understand this relationship and it makes me feel awkward. She is my boss, so I don't want to confront her, but I find the situation stressful. I like my job and I don't want to leave, but it looks like the only solution.'

MY SOLUTION

Don't hand in your letter of resignation yet. Your situation isn't as hopeless as you think.

This woman is clearly threatened by you in some way and needs to boost her own self-esteem by making you look incompetent. I would say the first thing is to understand that it's probably not personal, given that you get along well when the big brass isn't around. However, in the presence of senior staff, she does seem to need to make herself look superior at your expense. But you're more powerful than you think. Doing nothing is only robbing you of your confidence, so burying your head in the sand is no solution.

Your advantage here is that you have a good relationship with your boss outside of these meetings. Before your next meeting, you might want to have a brief chat with your boss and find out what the business agenda is. That way, she can find out what's going to be discussed and you can sound out her views on the matter. Since you'll now know her views, you can act in one of two ways. You can either go in agreeing with her or you can voice your opinions. The first option is safer, but the second will be less problematic, because at least you'll know what her potential criticisms are. Forewarned is forearmed.

Since you appear to like this woman, I would also suggest that you try to boost her confidence a bit by letting her know how much you enjoy working with her. This way, she'll see that you're part of her team and will feel less threatened by you.

Effective Leadership

Whether you want to set up on your own or rise through the ranks of a big corporation, you will need to stand out as a leader. Sometimes insecurities, low self-esteem or natural shyness mean people lack the confidence to promote themselves as leaders in the workplace. However, if the idea of heading a group of people or directing a course of action fills you with dread, there's no need to panic. Leaders aren't just born, they can also be made.

Many people who are not accustomed to adopting a leadership role will be surprised to find out that they are already equipped with many of the skills and resources they need. While any new skills will require practice, once you begin incorporating them into your routine, your new-found expertise will lead to further achievement and a true sense of mastery. Taking a leading role will be demanding and won't always be easy. You will face pressure, stress and conflicting demands.

However, in accepting the rough with the smooth, you will gain the respect of others.

What Do We Mean by Leadership?

A leader is someone who is able to build solid relationships with others, effectively use available resources, motivate people with his or her vision for a particular outcome, take responsibility when mistakes occur, encourage team members to participate and contribute ideas and be flexible in each situation.

Before we continue, I want you to take a few moments and think about someone who embodies the qualities of good leadership. Once you've done that, think about a person who demonstrates bad leadership traits. How do these two people differ?

Now, think of two situations in which you acted as a leader. This could be at work, at home, with your secretary or your children. It doesn't matter. I just want you to identify one circumstance in which your leadership was successful and another that proved less effective. How did these two situations differ for you?

Leaders come in all shapes and sizes. We can all draw on our personal and professional experience to offer direction to others. Leadership is not synonymous with dictatorship – not any more. Once upon a time, leaders were akin to autocrats. Theirs was the old 'when-I-want-your-opinion-I'll-give-it-to-you' style of management. While a few of those old codgers still exist, thankfully times have moved on. Nowadays, more and more organizations encourage a more co-operative approach to leadership and the old us-against-them attitudes are becoming increasingly rare.

Autocratic vs Co-operative Leadership

Autocratic: *It's my way or the highway.*

Co-operative: *I welcome everyone's contribution.*

Autocratic: *Seeking advice from subordinates is a sign of weakness.*

Co-operative: *Seeking advice from subordinates is a sign of strength.*

Autocratic: *The gains reflect me and my efforts only.*

Co-operative: *The gains reflect the team's efforts.*

Autocratic: *Authority will be undermined if other people have their say.*

Co-operative: *Authority will be strengthened by taking the concerns of subordinates seriously and encouraging their ideas, input and resources.*

Autocratic: *People are only brought on-side if you threaten them with 'the stick' approach.*

Co-operative: *People work together if you dangle a carrot in front of them.*

Autocratic: *I apply the same strategy to every situation.*

Co-operative: *I'm flexible and adapt my style according to each new situation.*

I certainly know which leadership style I'd prefer to work with!

Help with Leading Others

Learning effective leadership skills takes time, practice and dedication. And there is no substitute for hard graft. In time, you'll discover the approaches that work for you. You'll also tease out those which get you nowhere.

There are only two main pointers for developing new skills as a leader. You'll need to encourage team cohesiveness, and learn how to delegate tasks to others.

Developing Team Cohesion

Even the sturdiest of chains is only as strong as its weakest link. Remember this metaphor and you will be well on your way to establishing a solid, cohesive team. Group cohesion can be achieved by first deciding the identity of the team. People favour clubs and organizations with positive identities and reputations. Membership in a prestigious group reflects well on the individual. When people feel they belong to a highly regarded and well-respected organization, they flourish.

So maybe you'll want your team to be dynamic, energetic and creative. Or perhaps your vision reflects more of a traditional, conservative image. It doesn't matter. What's important is establishing your team's identity, very early on. And, I mean first thing. Once accomplished, your colleagues will have a better understanding of their role and your expectations of them.

Establishing your team's identity isn't daunting; it's actually very easy. You can achieve this by outlining your group's mission statement, values and rules. Maybe you have a firm idea of how you see this identity, but you might also want to open up the discussion to the group and brainstorm ideas.

With a clearer understanding of the group's identity, you should next set about encouraging group members to get to know each other. The development of good relationships among your colleagues will help strengthen their commitment to the group. Not only will your team have a better understanding of their own roles and how they are expected to relate to their colleagues, they'll begin to see how the project will take shape. As a result, you will inspire confidence and enthusiasm and your co-workers will feel more involved in and responsible for the project.

Delegation

With a strong sense of team cohesion now firmly developed, your next task as leader will be to assign specific duties and responsibilities.

Not everyone is comfortable with delegating. Particularly when people are new to leadership roles, their lack of experience may prompt them to become overly involved. While it's understandable to be concerned about the success of a project, avoid the temptation to hover. Your team members will only feel undermined, frustrated and resentful. Once their roles have been assigned, it's better to encourage the group to work independently. Basically, just let them get on with it.

Remember, you're not there to hold someone's hand or to do the job for them. Your role is to oversee the project and make yourself available should problems arise.

There are four basic rules to delegating effectively. Follow them, and you will find your confidence in your abilities soaring.

TAKE TIME TO DISCUSS THE WORK INVOLVED

In busy organizations and offices everywhere, time is as valuable as it is rare. However, when you're establishing a new team and assigning roles for a project, you cannot afford to scrimp. Taking the time and making yourself available to discuss relevant issues such as role assignments, budget, deadlines, resources and goals will eliminate misunderstandings and delays. Furthermore, when colleagues are fully informed about the project and their role, from an early stage they will feel more involved, committed and enthusiastic about their work.

EXPLAIN WHY EACH PERSON'S ROLE IS IMPORTANT

Studies have shown that people perform better at their jobs if they understand the purpose of their role and are told how their work fits in with the big picture. Working in isolation on a meaningless task doesn't exactly inspire enthusiasm. In contrast, linking one job with those of co-workers in the context of a common goal encourages people to pull together.

We can see evidence of this phenomenon outside the workplace as well. Psychologists have found that people are more willing to obey instructions when they are given good reason for doing so. Signs informing us 'Please keep quiet. Exam in progress,' 'Keep off grass. Re-seeding in progress,' 'Don't feed the pigeons. They've become a menace' promote co-operation because they explain and refer to the common purpose and general benefit behind the restriction.

SPECIFY YOUR EXPECTATIONS

People aren't mind-readers. We can only live up to someone else's standards if we know what they are. This point may seem obvious, but even experienced managers often make assumptions that their colleagues intuitively know what is expected of them. Is it any wonder that mistakes are made? Or that delays arise? Just think: Can your professional reputation afford such disasters?

The moral is: Be very clear about your expectations. Asking yourself the following questions is a good place to start.

- *How will you evaluate your colleague?*
- *What are the limits of their authority on a project?*
- *How often do you expect to be updated on developments?*
- *How would you define your role in relation to that of your co-worker?*

ASSESSING THE OUTCOME

Once a project is complete, you will need to evaluate the roles and performance of everyone involved. In doing so, you will be able to clarify those factors that made the project a success and identify those that need improvement.

If you've followed the previous steps, however, then this job will be a cinch. While most people feel uncomfortable when they're being appraised, if you've been clear about expectations from the start, then the evaluation process will be fair. If, instead, you spring your assessment criteria on your colleagues only after the job is finished, people will feel undermined and resentful. Understandably.

> *Kate worked for a company who weren't very clear about their expectations. For six months she had worked on a report and made sure she gave regular feedback to her project manager. Since she was never given any suggestions for improvement, Kate carried on. So it came as a complete surprise when, upon completion, her boss criticized the report and questioned her ability to take on the responsibility.*
>
> *Kate felt confused and demeaned. She couldn't understand why these points weren't mentioned earlier. In failing to work closely with and guide her, Kate's boss let both her and the company down. In a big way. Kate felt unsupported and wary of future involvement in the company. She left at the first possible opportunity.*

At the end of the day, leadership is mainly about managing people and ensuring that they work effectively together for a common goal. Successful leadership will encourage people to feel motivated, able and enthusiastic about investing their efforts on a project. When leadership is unsuccessful, colleagues will feel undermined, de-skilled and will probably begin looking for employment elsewhere.

Taking on the Role of Leader

Next week, I want you to put your new leadership skills into practice. Whether you agree to take on extra responsibilities at work, co-ordinate a social event at your club or organize your children as they clean out the cellar, it doesn't matter. Leadership comes in many forms.

Once you've completed the task, take a minute to find out how successful your efforts were:

- *What were you hoping to accomplish?*
- *What did you find personally rewarding about the experience?*
- *How did you motivate others to follow your plan?*
- *In what ways did you address any problems that arose?*
- *How successful were you at delegating?*
- *How did you handle conflict?*
- *How did the other people involved respond to your leadership role?*
- *In what way(s) were you successful?*
- *What areas need improvement?*

The SWOT Analysis

Now that you've read this book and reflected more on your own experiences, I think you'll benefit from another SWOT analysis. Reassess your strengths, weaknesses, opportunities and threats in the light of what you've now learned about yourself.

SWOT Analysis

MY STRENGTHS

1.
2.
3.
4.
5.

MY WEAKNESSES

1.
2.
3.
4.
5.

OPPORTUNITIES	THREATS
1.	1.
2.	2.
3.	3.
4.	4.
5.	5.

In what ways are your responses similar to the earlier SWOT? How are they different?

Index